Contents

Editorial Foreword

Classes and status groups are, in Weber's phrase, 'phenomena of the distribution of power in a community'. But they are also manifestations of what Durkheim called a society's 'moral classification of men and things', which is ultimately a 'religious' phenomenon. The study of stratification, then, involves an understanding of society as a totality: its economy polity and its system of values and beliefs. Each form of stratification has a legal basis (even when this is one of formal equality of citizenship); it has its own 'political economy'; its own ideological rationale. These conditions determine the extent of class antagonisms and the degree of solidification of status structures; and such variations in the shape of stratification from one society to another constitute the main subject matter of this branch of sociology. Underlying these variations, however, basically similar forces are at work. Societies are systems distinguished by their peculiar need for solidarity and their occasional liability to schism. And because social stratification is uniquely expressive of these fundamental alternations of consensus and disorder in society as a whole, it is the object of sociological study *par excellence*. Unequal and never wholly stable distributions of goods and power are the source of an ever present potential for conflict the actualization of which is contrary to the nature of a status hierarchy which seeks to legitimize privilege and disadvantage and to generate wants in accordance with its own moral matrix. This regulation is always imperfect, partly because the accumulation and dissolution of power has a momentum which is inconsiderate of established expectancies of status. Newly created power has a hunger for legitimation in a status order that is congruent with its own structure just as status, once formed, endeavours to appropriate nascent power which might threaten its authorization of inequality. But the regulation is also imperfect because the logic of status reaches beyond the world of inequality as it finds it and to which it must accommodate. Its horizons are ideal, and the tension between ideology and reality is an additional reason why adherence to a status order is never unconditional, even on the part of those who are most indulged by its dispensation. Indeed, the tendency of status hierarchies to call forth their own negation in the ideal of equality is very widespread. In many cases, the influence of this ideal has been only very feeble, peripheral and intermittent; but in some it has become the central activating principle of massive social change – thereby adding the 'sociology of classlessness' to the agenda of the study of stratification.

David Lane's book addresses itself directly to this latter problem by posing the question: has inequality been abolished in state-socialist societies? His answer provides the interpretation by a diversity of factual material relating to the social structure of the Soviet Union (as well as other societies in Eastern Europe following its political model); and, at the same time, he sets up the unusually explicit theory which that society has about itself. Dr Lane conveys his specialist knowledge of the subject in a style which will make his work accessible to a wider audience than just students of sociology.

David Lockwood

Preface

I am indebted to Professor David Lockwood and to my wife whose suggestions have considerably improved the text. My work has also benefited from comments made by students at Essex University who have been exposed to some of the chapters when given as lectures.

Acknowledgement is made to the following for permission to use copyright material: University of Chicago Press; Polish Scientific Publishers; Pall Mall Press; Professor Bogdar Denitch (for International Study of Opinion-Makers); Dr S. Bieler; Mr K. Slomczynski; Central Statistical Office, Warsaw; Central Statistical Office, Budapest.

Throughout the book words have been anglicized to the extent of omitting all diacritical signs.

Introduction

From time immemorial radicals have opposed inequality. Thinkers have advocated the redistribution of wealth from the rich to the poor, of power from the rulers to the exploited. Radical men of action have sought to change society from a state of what they see as degradation to one where any man's rights, possessions, power and honour are equal to the next man's. But to abolish or reduce such inequality requires more than moral platitudes. Why do men inherit a world of inequality, what are its causes, how does one abolish them? The politician and sociologist make different assumptions about the causes of inequality. The former is constrained in his appraisal by his political interests and by those of his supporters, whereas the sociologist, who may also often be committed to social change, attempts to formulate his analysis in more general terms by establishing laws about social structures and their transformation. The experience of the Soviet Union is particularly relevant to these problems, because in October 1917 the Bolsheviks attempted to lay the foundation stones for a society in which men would live in harmony and equality. The October Revolution was not concerned with the amelioration of conditions in Tsarist Russia from the viewpoint of liberal ideas of distributive justice, but with changing the fundamental structure of power and authority. How far have the Communists succeeded in their quest? Have they found that immutable social laws have turned to stone their good intentions? Were the Marxist theories which the Russian Bolsheviks used to justify their action false, or were they betrayed by men whose political interests debased these ideals? It is hoped that this study of social stratification of state-socialist society may provide some of the answers to these questions.

'State socialist' is a label used to describe societies, modelled on the Soviet Union, which are distinguished by a state-owned, a more or less centrally controlled, planned economy and by a politically dominant communist party. At the same time, the cultural and social orders of such states exhibit considerable variation and it has been found impossible to cover their diversity in a short text. The Soviet Union, of course, occupies a dominant political position in Eastern Europe and it is also sociologically interesting because the communists have been in power there for much longer than in other countries. Therefore it has been taken as the main subject of study except when discussing some topics where the paucity of source materials on the Soviet Union has made it necessary to refer to research carried out in other Eastern European countries. I have tried to give a balanced picture of both Western and 'indigenous' research. Much of the empirical research (both Western and state socialist) is deficient in that results of surveys are often given only in percentage form, the sampling is not truly representative of the population described, the questions put are ambiguous and the categories used by the researchers in analysing data are inadequately defined. But making the best of such empirical research is the only way of going beyond vague generalities and speculations and approximating to a sociology of state-socialist society.

In a short text of this kind it is impossible to give a full descriptive account of the many facets of social stratification in Soviet society. I have tried to interweave theoretical, historical and contemporary aspects of Soviet society to show how Marxist ideology has influenced the official description of Soviet reality and to show how Marx's views of class have been adapted to describe the dictatorship of the proletariat and the Soviet notion of a socialist society. The most important issue here is the relevance of Marx's notion of class to the actual structure of power after the Bolshevik Revolution. In chapter 1 are described the original views of Marx and their adaptation by Soviet Communists in the description of Russia before and after the Revolution. This involves a brief historical review of Soviet developments between 1917 and 1956: a contrast between the class structure of Tsarist Russia and the dictatorship of the proletariat (between 1917 and 1936) and an examination of the first stage of Soviet socialism (1936 to 1956). However, not wishing to restrict the study to a *Soviet* Marxist framework, I have outlined other approaches to Soviet society. In chapter 2 several different models of the Soviet social order are discussed: here are considered both Marxist critics of the Soviet theory of class relations (Trotsky, Schachtman, Kuron and Modzelewski) and totalitarian theorists (Aron, Kornhauser and Arendt). In chapters 3 to 5 empirical research on social stratification in mainly post-1956 Soviet (and East European) society is summarized. Much of this work considers status and hierarchy rather than class in a Marxist sense. These chapters also review the literature which has sought to make comparisons between the structure of Eastern European societies and Western capitalist ones, as well as other studies of social hierarchy and political inequality in state-socialist society. Finally, in the conclusion, some generalizations about stratification stemming from the experience of state-socialist society are put forward.

The arrangement of the text facilitates the discussion of three interrelated problems of social stratification as they apply to state-socialist societies. Firstly, there is the relevance of the Marxist notion of *class*, by which we mean a social and economic group differentiated by its 'relationship to the means of production' with a common political interest against other classes. Class in this sense is a tool in the analysis of history, a causal factor in the transformation of societies. The important question here is the nature of the political structure of a society in which classes in the formal Marxist sense have been abolished. This is the subject-matter of chapters 1 and 2. Secondly, we are concerned with the nature of *social inequality* in a state-socialist society. Social inequality refers to the uneven distribution of goods and values among the population in the sense that one group may have more income or education than another; and this aspect of stratification is the concern of chapter 3. Closely connected to inequality is the *ranking* and *privilege* of individuals or groups on a scale of superiority or inferiority; and these are the topics of chapter 4. In chapter 5 we examine the related question of the extent to which individual statuses are available to open recruitment or conversely are restricted to certain groups.

1 The Impact of Marxist Ideas in Russia before and after the October Revolution

Marxism and the pre-revolutionary background

The first aspect of stratification mentioned above was that of class and the main task of this chapter is to explain what role class played in Marx's theory, how his ideas were developed by his followers in Tsarist Russia and how later they were adapted to the structure of the Soviet Union.

In the original theory of Marx, class occupied the centre of the stage as the prime mover of historical development. Classes were social entities formed on the basis of economic relations. Ownership relations were the prime, though not exclusive, deter inants of class position.

What makes wage labourers, capitalists and landlords constitute the three great classes?

At first glance – the identity of revenues and sources of revenue. There are three great social groups whose members, the individuals forming them, live on wages, profit and ground rent respectively, on the realization of their labour power, their capital and their landed property (Marx, 1867, pp. 862–3).

The relationship to the means of production, or market relations, was the basis on which classes, the chief agents of history, were formed. Mrax was less concerned with the other two elements of social stratification mentioned above, inequality and ranking. To be sure, they are related: the ruling class, by virtue of its economic power, has in the eyes of many, high prestige or honour; and the exploited has what might be called a low and congruent ranking in terms of power, income and status. 'State-socialist' Marxists have tended to concentrate attention on the element of property relations inherent in Marxist thought and have applied this rather mechanically to power relations and social stratification.

Marx concentrated on explaining the inner logic of social change and emphasized that social transformations could not take place independently of the economic structure. But ownership relations are only one part of the economic basis, the other being the forces of production, that is the character of technology or the kind of tools (including intellectual ones) which are utilized at a certain stage of development. Marx describes the relationship of social transformation to economic structure and the conditions of social transformation in two well-known passages. He says:

No social order ever perishes before all the productive forces for which there is room in it have developed; and new, higher relations of production never appear before the material conditions for their existence have matured in the womb of the old society itself (1958b, p. 363). [He also wrote] Men make their own history, but they do not make it just as they please; they do not make it under circumstances chosen by themselves, but under circumstances directly encountered, given and transmitted from the past (1958a, p. 247).

While the conflict of economic classes dominates history, the characteristics of the ruling and exploited classes will depend on the technological level of development of the society.[1] Social transformations are limited therefore by the level of technological advance, and political action must be related to the development of the productive forces. If we interpret Marx literally, a communist society without social classes would necessarily follow the capitalist form, for only after this stage would the technology be able to sustain economic abundance. Let us now consider how well Russia fitted into his scheme.

In the late nineteenth and early twentieth century, the Russian Empire did not fit conveniently into any one of Marx's ideal types. It could be said to contain elements of feudal and bourgeois societies. It was feudal in the sense that

1. Marx defined five 'ideal type' societies: Asiatic (or primitive communism), ancient, feudal, bourgeois and communist (1958b, vol. 1, p. 363). These may be regarded as the main forms of civilization: ancient society was characterized by the ownership of slaves, feudal society had a ruling class which possessed land, in bourgeois society the capitalist class owned the large-scale enterprises producing economic wealth and in communist society no classes would exist.

the chief form of production was a manorial type of agriculture on which rested the ruling landowning class, the basis of Tsarist power. But in addition industrial capitalism was making great strides: a railway system and other communications and large-scale industrial complexes were set up in many parts of Russia.[2] Peculiar features of this economic development were, on the one hand, the absence of a dynamic indigenous bourgeoisie in the sense of private owners of the means of production and, on the other hand, the presence of a modern proletariat. The Russian bourgeoisie was small and ineffective and industrial development had been sponsored by the Russian government. In the late nineteenth century much industry was either formally government-owned and controlled, or foreign-owned and subsidized by the state. The proletariat – factory and mining workers – numbered some two and a half million in 1913 out of a total population of 139 millions. Those drawing a wage or salary from any source accounted for 16·7 per cent of the population, and another 7·2 per cent were handicraftsmen employed on their own account. Though the industrial proletariat was small, industrial enterprises were large: whereas 53 per cent of Russian workers were employed in factories with five hundred or more men, in the USA at the same time (1910) only 33 per cent were so employed.

The crucial characteristics of Russian society then were that the capitalist mode of production was present only in embryo form and the indigenous capitalist class was weak. In so far as the latter did exist, it was protected by the 'feudal' powers. The proletariat, which was recruited from the oppressed peasantry, was being organized in Marxist parties which had a greater influence in the nascent working class in Russia than in the more slowly developing Western European societies. One of the reasons for this was that almost any kind of political association was banned in Russia. 'Gradualist' political parties and trade unions did not develop to the same extent as in other capitalist countries and in their absence it was not

2. Industrial production increased five-fold between 1885 and 1913. See comparative figures in Gerschenkron (1947, p. 156).

possible for the working class to be 'incorporated' into the regime. Increasingly they turned instead to the leadership of illegal Marxist revolutionary groups.

Faced with this situation, 'classical' and 'radical' Marxists came to fundamentally different conclusions about the course of social change in Russia. The 'classical' school, epitomized by the Mensheviks, thought that the proletariat could play a small part in bringing about a *bourgeois* revolution. Until this had been achieved and until the bourgeoisie had transformed feudal Russia into a modern industrial state, all talk of socialism or of the 'dictatorship of the proletariat' was premature and inimical to the interests of the working class. The workers, they argued, should form as wide a trade-union type of party as conditions would allow. The 'radicals' (Lenin and the Bolsheviks) regarded this view either as 'revisionist' or as a formalist interpretation of Marx. In Russian conditions, they said, the traditional form of social-democratic party was impractical. A select party of Marxists, led by professional revolutionaries, was apposite to Russian conditions. In Russia, they believed, a socialist revolution was possible. They argued that capitalism should be analysed as a world economic system, which the First World War brought to explosion point. In 1917, only a spark was needed. That spark could be kindled in the country where capitalism was weakest and proletarian organization strongest – in Russia. The proletariat, therefore, should not passively wait for the full development of a bourgeois society, for it was doubtful if the Russian bourgeoisie had sufficient class consciousness to fulfil its historic role. The correct course for the Russian working class of this view was to abolish the autocratic system and seize political power, then, after completing their own revolution, the victorious proletariat in the advanced countries would help secure a communist system in Russia.

These ideas help one to understand the nature of social and political change in Soviet Russia after the Bolshevik seizure of power in October 1917. The uprising of the advanced Western proletariat did not materialize and the Soviet government found itself ruling in one of the economically most underdeveloped and backward countries in Europe. In a Marxist sense, *politically* the ruling class was now the proletariat, but the society over which it ruled was not socialist: it could not strictly speaking be *de facto* a socialist society because the economic forces had not outgrown the technological level of the capitalist stage of production. After seizing political power, Lenin and the Russian Communist Party[3] consciously set out to complete two tasks involving the transformation of the society inherited after the revolution. These were first, the destruction of the system of social classes inherited from Tsarist Russia, and second, the creation of a system of social relations embodying the new socialist order.

Soviet Marxists have distinguished four distinct historical phases in the development of Soviet society:

1. October 1917 to 1925: a period of social revolution.
2. 1926 to 1936: years of socialist industrialization.
3. 1936 to 1956: the epoch in which the first phase of building socialism was completed.
4. 1956 to the present: the second phase of socialist construction, the building of communist society (*Marksistsko-leninskaya filosofiya i sotsiologiya v SSSR i Evropeiskikh sotsialisticheskikh stran*, 1965 pp. 8–9).

In Marxist-Leninist terms, these four historical stages may be combined into two analytically distinct societies: the phase of the dictatorship of the proletariat (1917 to 1936); and the building of socialist society (1936 to the present). The chief theoretical distinction between these societies from the Soviet Marxist viewpoint lies in the character of class relations, for while the dictatorship of the proletariat still entailed class conflict, socialist society did not.

3. The name, Russian Communist Party (Bolsheviks), was adopted in 1918; before this time the Bolsheviks operated as a faction of the Russian Social-Democratic Labour Party. In 1952 the name of the party was changed to Communist Party of the Soviet Union.

The social structure of the 'dictatorship of the proletariat'

In *Leninist theory*, the downfall of the Tsarist Empire ushered in neither 'socialism' nor 'communism'. The immediate task of the Bolsheviks was to ensure the rule of the proletariat: rather than being democratic, the political structure was defined officially as the 'dictatorship of the proletariat'. This was justified on the grounds that the working class had to defend itself against a possible counter-revolution. The social structure of the 'dictatorship of the proletariat' involved a polarization of classes: on one side was the proletariat in a 'friendly alliance' (*smychka*) with the peasantry, on the other was the bourgeoisie and the aristocracy.

This world view shaped the Bolsheviks' immediate social policy. The changes which followed the seizure of political power by the Bolsheviks were introduced gradually, rather than in one fell swoop. Within a year after the Revolution of 1917, decrees had been passed nationalizing the land and the key industries – coal, oil, iron, steel, chemicals and textiles. By December 1920 nationalization was extended to all enterprises employing more than five workers using any kind of mechanical power or to those employing more than ten without mechanical power. These measures coupled with laws restricting inheritance, were an attack on the landlords and capitalists. The dispossession of the ownership-based classes was paralleled by the loss of position and privileges of other previously dominant groups. All titles and ranks were abolished. Many senior state bureaucrats were dismissed; church and state were separated. The members of the previous ruling classes lost their civic rights; they could not vote or join the Communist Party. There was a period of intense class struggle: the large estates were seized and split up among independent peasant proprietors. Members of the technical and administrative strata, whose previous class position identified them with the possessing classes, were 'declassed' and made to work, as it were, for the proletariat. They lost their privileges, their salaries were significantly reduced, often their houses were shared with the poor, and during the periods of food rationing they received 'according to their work' which in practice often meant the lowest grade of ration card (Lenin, 1965, p. 107–17). These socially-levelling or 'egalitarian' policies were seen as meeting the demands of the class struggle. They were essentially *class* changes.

But side by side with such attacks on the old order, other more constructive measures were introduced by the Bolsheviks and these also affected social stratification and inequality. Wages were equalized (see pp. 30–32) and other measures removed various forms of discrimination and advantage which were prevalent before the Revolution. Women were given equal legal rights with men. Campaigns were conducted to make the population literate. Polytechnical education, involving all children in manual and mental work, was advocated as a means of reducing the social distance between the various kinds of labour. The educational system, dedicated to the development of a new communist man, was organized on child-centred non-authoritarian principles.

In addition to such 'planned' equalitarianism, the early years of the Revolution were ones of turmoil, and although the Communist Party was ostensibly the vanguard of the proletariat, it was not always in control. In this situation the workers 'introduced communism' by instituting workers' control and the inflation was seen by some as the beginning of an era of free goods. It need hardly be added that the latter had nothing to do with the social theory of the Bolsheviks but was a result of the chaos of revolution and civil war.

Yet despite the measures directed against it, the bourgeoisie as a class was not completely obliterated. After the period of Civil War (1917–22), small factories, retail trade and almost the whole of agricultural production remained under private management and produced surplus for profit. The Bolshevik government's edict nationalizing the land had occurred concurrently with the small proprietory peasantry seizing and splitting up the large estates. Consequently, they worked the land in the form of private plots and traded their surplus with the towns. Thus, until the collectivization of agriculture in

1929, a large area of private enterprise and bourgeois values prevailed and in the countryside the Bolsheviks had not yet a wide social basis of political support.

The Bolsheviks' social legislation was also directed against other important institutions of the old social structure. The Russian patriarchal family was held to embody bourgeois values and to be an element conserving the old regime. The government's early decrees were therefore designed to undermine this institution. The fact of cohabitation and a common household became recognized as marriage. Divorce was easily obtainable by either spouse and the legal status of husband and wife was made equal before the courts. Children born outside registered marriage were given the same rights with regard to their parents as children born of it. In general, Soviet family legislation in this period succeeded in weakening parental authority.

Even during the immediate post-revolutionary period, it is noteworthy that many features of the old regime were retained. Industrial discipline was based on a hierarchical management pattern and syndicalism and workers' management of production were repudiated. The monogamous family, albeit in a weakened form, was preserved and sexual licence was deplored. It must be made clear that it was *not* the intention of the Bolsheviks to abolish the wage system or to introduce the equal distribution of commodities as advocated by Anarchists (Kropotkin, 1888). We shall see later that high wage differentials also characterized Soviet Russia under a later phase of the 'dictatorship of the proletariat'.

The relatively underdeveloped state of the country and the Bolsheviks' expectation that the intervention of the advanced West European proletariat was imminent, are reasons why 'socialism' was not immediately introduced. In this initial period, the 'dictatorship of the proletariat' was regarded as a transitionary and temporary one.

By the mid 1920s, however, the Soviet leaders came to accept that the Western proletariat would not complete a successful revolution against the bourgeoisie, and the Russian

Communists turned therefore to create a socio-economic base which would secure their rule. The original justification of the Revolution in October 1917 was that it was the *first step* towards the establishment of, in Lenin's words, 'a socialist organization of society and the victory of socialism in all countries'. But in 1926, Stalin argued that the first stage of communism, the 'socialist' stage, could be completed in Russia 'without the preliminary victory of the proletarian revolution in other countries'. Social change of a more radical kind was envisaged in the USSR after Stalin's statement: it included the obliteration of what were regarded as the remaining bourgeois strata, the small-holding peasantry, and the creation of a large working class and 'communist' intelligentsia. This was the second phase of the 'dictatorship of the proletariat'.

Industrialization and collectivization

The expropriation of the large capitalist magnates and landed gentry in the early years of the Revolution had been carried out relatively easily, for it had widespread popular support and these strata made up a small proportion of the population. The problem of the small-holding peasantry was quite a different matter, for in 1928 there were some twenty-five million individual peasant farms. Moreover, the October Revolution had been carried out, according to official Leninist theory, by an alliance between the proletariat and the peasantry which was founded on hostility of both these groups to the autocracy, big landowners and the magnates of capital. But the individual plot-farming peasant did not have a proletarian socialist ideology. The peasant's mentality was conditioned by tradition. He sought to realize his long held aspirations for individual proprietory rights and wanted to preserve his firm attachment to the soil. After 1917 and the seizure of the land, the class interests of the peasantry, in so far as it sought private production for profit, were inimical to the ruling Communist Party. Had the Russian Revolution spread to the West, governments representing the European proletariat might have supported the Russian Communists with economic aid and the 'peasant problem' might have been slowly resolved. But the Russian Communists had to deal with the problem alone. They did so by a policy of collectivization which involved the expropriation of most of the peasant small-holdings and the creation of *kolkhozy*, or collective farms, which brought the land under the administrative control of the Bolshevik government. One of the most momentous changes in modern times involved the transfer of peasant plots, stock and seeds to collective farms. When the collectivization drive began in 1929, only 3·9 per cent of households had been collectivized but by 1938, 93·5 per cent of them were so organized. Behind these figures lies a story of the seizure of peasant property and of the extermination, or transportation to Siberia, of an estimated five million peasants.

The second strand in Stalin's policy of building a socialist society in Soviet Russia was rapid industrialization which was carried out in the first two Five-Year Plans (1928–32; 1933–7). Except to note that the Soviet average annual rate of growth of all industry between 1928 and 1932 has been estimated at 20·35 per cent (Gerschenkron, 1947, p. 161), the details of this economic development need not detain us here. Rapid industrialization did involve, however, a dramatic change in the occupational structure. Between 1928 and 1937 the number of manual and non-manual workers employed in industry rose from 3·8 to 10·1 millions – a two and a half-fold increase. In heavy industry, the number of manual workers more than doubled between 1929 and 1936, rising from 2·8 millions to 6·2 millions (Rashin, 1961, pp. 16, 29). Similarly, the urban population rose from 19 per cent of the total in 1929 to 33 per cent in 1940 (Tsentral'noe statisticheskoe upravlenie, 1963; 1966).

The official Soviet figures which summarize the main changes are shown on Table 1. Whereas in 1913, 83 per cent of the population was self-employed (peasants or bourgeoisie) by 1939 manual and non-manual workers accounted for about half of the population, the number of self-employed peasants and craftsmen had dwindled to some 3 per cent, and the bour-

Table 1 Social Structure of Soviet Population 1913, 1928, 1939 (Official figures)

	1913	1928	1939
Manual and non-manual workers	17	17	50
Collective-farm peasantry and craftsmen	0	3	47
Independent peasants and craftsmen	67	75	3
Bourgeoisie, landowners, merchants, *kulaks* (rich independent peasants)	16	5	0
Total (including non-working members of families)	100	100	100

Source: Tsentral'noe Statisticheskoe upravlenie (1966, p. 42). In absolute terms the number of employed manual and non-manual workers rose from 11·4 millions in 1913 to 62 millions in 1960 and by 1968 they totalled 85·1 millions. The number of employed non-manuals increased from 2·9 millions in 1926 to 20·5 million in 1959 and 29·9 million in 1968 (Tsentral'noe statisticheskoe upravlenie, 1969, pp. 35, 547).

geoisie no longer existed.[4] Let us now turn to consider the political relations which lie behind these figures.

After the October Revolution, the working class was in theory the ruling class sustaining the dictatorship of the proletariat. This concept gives rise to a number of political and social problems at various levels of power. A ruling class cannot rule by controlling or occupying only the elite positions, it must ensure also that many other posts of authority are filled by politically reliable men. In an industrial society such positions require training in specific skills and techniques. Here the Bolsheviks were in a dilemma for most of the technical specialists inherited from Tsarist Russia were either of bourgeois social extraction, or regarded themselves as bourgeois, and such men, it was thought, could not be trusted to

4. It is worth pointing out that occupational change in England and Wales has followed a similar trend. In the nineteenth century the main shift from the country to the town occurred: between 1911 and 1951 the numbers of employers and self-employed drastically declined, those of the professions and skilled labour rose (Hobsbawm, 1968, diagrams 8–12).

work conscientiously for the new rulers. On the other hand, the main supporters of the Communist Party – the urban proletariat – had neither the education nor the skill necessary to man the command posts of the society.

The Communist government solved this problem in two ways: firstly, by political sanctions and a policy of political placement; and secondly, by a crash programme of education. Political sanctions involved the use of terror as a mechanism to ensure conformity to the will of the political elite. This was directed against those strata who were thought to be sympathetic to the dispossessed classes. As early as July 1918, Lenin had said that Soviet power had to be guaranteed 'by putting the bourgeoisie under suspicion and carrying out mass terror against it' (see Carr, 1950, p. 167). Carr sums up Bolshevik policy as follows: 'The essence of the terror was its class character. It selected its victims on the ground, not of specific offences, but of their membership of the possessing classes' (p. 168). The fear of arrest, imprisonment or death was used not only to deter a counter-revolutionary rising, but to make the population adaptable and amenable to the communist political elites. In addition to these measures, political commissars were appointed to the Red Army with power to countermand orders. Even though the technical control of industrial enterprises had to be left in the hands of the pre-revolutionary bourgeois specialists,[5] 'Red Directors' were appointed to supervise their activity and to ensure that they did not sabotage the communist political order (Bienstock, Schwartz and Yugow, 1948, ch. 1). At higher levels of economic administration, the authorities had succeeded as early as 1927 in promoting sufficient Communist Party members to guarantee control of the industrial trusts. By that year, 65 per cent of their members at director level and 98 per cent of the chairmen were party members (Drobizhev, 1961, p. 63).

During this process the Communist Party underwent a transformation. From being a secret underground party of revolutionaries, it now became a ruling body. Its members ex-

5. In 1925, for example, only 1·3 per cent of technical factory chiefs were communists (Drobizhev, 1961, p. 64).

perienced upward social mobility. We may appreciate the magnitude of this change by examining the composition of the party before and after the Revolution. There can be no doubt that the leaders of the Bolshevik party before the Revolution were from the educated middle social strata. Of the fifty-one delegates at the party's founding congress in 1903 only three had been workers, though later (1907) their number rose to over half of the 218 delegates. At the lower levels of the party, the Bolshevik activists were largely recruited from the working class (Lane, 1969). The social origins of the leaders may be clearly seen by studying Table 2, which shows the membership of the party's central committee. These were the men who later experienced rapid upward mobility from lower–middle status groups to the apex of the power structure after 1917. It is pertinent to note the very small number of workers in the party elite, and the figures cited include not one peasant. At the lower levels of the party, workers predominated: in 1905 and in 1917, they constituted some 60 per cent of the total membership, but peasants made up only from 5 to 8 per cent (Bubnov, 1930, col. 533).

Table 2

Social Origin of Bolshevik Party Elite, 1903–18

Party congress	Social origin of central committee as percentage	
	Manual workers	Non-manual
II 1903	0	100
III 1905	0	100
IV 1906	0	100
V 1907	6*	88*
VI 1917	12	88
VII 1918	21·7	78·3

* Excludes 1 of unknown social position

Source: Bubnov (1930, cols. 539–40).

After 1917, party membership grew. It rose from 115,000 on 1 January 1918 to 251,000 on 1 January 1919, and by March

1920, the party was 611,978 strong (Bubnov, 1930, col. 53). The majority of the new members were young, at the end of 1919 over half of the party's membership was aged under thirty. It was recruited from the previous underprivileged: 5 per cent had had higher education and 8 per cent secondary; 52 per cent had been employed as manual workers, 15 per cent as peasants and 18 per cent as non-manual workers.[6] These men provided the backbone of the new Soviet economic, administrative and political elites. By 1921, of 15,000 leading party officials, a third were of proletarian origin, the bulk of the others originated mainly from the lower-middle status groups (Schapiro, 1960, p. 237). Large numbers of men joined the party: membership rose from 350,000 in March 1919 to three and a half million in 1935 (Rigby, 1968, p. 52). From 1924 to 1932 the 'Lenin enrolment' attempted to give the party a fundamentally working-class complexion. Between 1922 and 1932, the proportion of those of manual-worker origin in the party increased from 44 per cent to 55 per cent and the share of men of non-manual-worker origin fell from 29 per cent to 8 per cent. But when one considers the actual occupations of party members, one sees that in 1932 some 38 per cent of the total membership was in non-manual work (Rigby, 1968, p. 116). This entailed considerable upward mobility by placement through the political system and involved the adoption of ascriptive criteria for social mobility.

The second means by which the Communist government prepared the working class for positions of authority was through special provision for the improvement of the educational standards of workers. 'Workers' faculties' were formed, usually attached to existing higher educational institutions: by 1921 there were fifty-nine faculties with 25,436 students (Katuntseva, 1966, p. 17). It has been estimated that between October 1917 and 1932 between 800,000 and 900,000 men were trained for the new 'Soviet intelligentsia' (Andreyuk, 1966, p. 38). In the sphere of admission to higher education, priority was given to children of proletarian and peasant social origins.

6. Figures cited by Schapiro (1960, pp. 233–4). For other statistics on the social composition of the Party see Semenov (1964, p. 257).

Whereas this group constituted 49·3 per cent of the intake to higher educational institutions in 1928, by 1931 the number had shot up to 65·6 per cent: in industrial institutes the respective figures were 52·9 per cent and 73·1 per cent (Drobizhev, 1961, p. 70). Despite these changes and the clear intentions of the Communist elites to change the social composition of institutes of higher learning to the detriment of the middle status groups and to the advantage of the workers and peasants, the 'class chances' of access to higher education were still very much in favour of the middle strata. Feldmesser has calculated that in the 1930s as a whole, 17·5 per cent of the Soviet population was non-manual, but 42·2 per cent of college students came from this group; manual workers were only slightly over-represented with 33·9 per cent of the students and 32·3 per cent of the total population; peasants, on the other hand, constituted 46·4 per cent of the population but only 21·7 per cent of the student body (1957, p. 94). Again De Witt has estimated that at the height of the 'proletarianization drive', 45 per cent of students in higher educational institutions were from the intelligentsia, which accounted for only 7 to 10 per cent of the total population (1961, p. 351). The Soviet figures cited earlier, therefore, are probably selective and not typical for the whole period.

These figures are in keeping with measures of occupational mobility for the inter-war period worked out on the basis of a survey of Russian *émigrés* by Miller (1960). On a comparative basis, Soviet working-class children (together with French) had the highest rate of *upward* social mobility, i.e. the sons of manual working-class fathers taking up non-manual occupations. The amount of *downward* social mobility was also found, in this sample, to be very low: non-manual into manual was 15 per cent, compared to 42·1 per cent in Great Britain. The amount of movement into the 'elite' occupational strata[7] was the highest of all the countries compared: 14·5 per cent in the USSR sample, compared to only 7·8 per cent in the USA. Despite this considerable upward mobility on the part of

7. Those occupational groups with very high social standing (Miller, 1960, p. 37).

working-class sons, Miller's comparative study shows that the advantages to Soviet middle-class sons (to improve or maintain status) were very similar to those in other countries (Denmark, France, Great Britain, Sweden and the USA) (Miller, 1960, p. 36).

We are now in a position to make a number of general points about stratification based on the history of Soviet Russia during her formative years. First, we must reject decisively the view of Bendix and Lipset that the implications for social mobility of the introduction of a new social system are not very important (1959, p. 282). The political apparatus in the first twenty years of Soviet power had a profound effect on the system of social stratification: it was responsible for the abolition of some social strata (the autocracy, the private rich peasantry); it instigated the recruitment of the previously deprived to positions of power and it was instrumental in advancing their occupational, educational and social standing. Secondly, the industrialization process itself required the recruitment of the most educable strata of the population. This entailed a modification of the Bolsheviks' policy of ascription and 'proletarianization'. Thirdly, the change of party role from that of an underground revolutionary body to that of a governing one, had the effect of promoting men from subordinate social positions to ruling ones.

At this point we may turn from the issue of political power and political relations to consider the extent of *economic* inequalities in the new Soviet order and to see in what ways, if any, the Communists reshaped the pattern of distribution.

Even in the early days of the Revolution, wage differentials between skilled and unskilled were recognized as necessary:

While aspiring to equality of remuneration for all kinds of labour and to total communism, the Soviet Government cannot consider as its task the immediate realization of this equality at the present moment when only the first steps are being made towards the transition from capitalism to communism (Baykov, 1947, p. 43).

Nevertheless, wage differentials were greatly reduced: in 1919, the *official* wage ratio between the highest and lowest grades of manual worker was $1\frac{3}{4}$:1 (Bergson, 1944, p. 182). But these policies were made irrelevant by the facts of the situation. In the immediate post-revolutionary period, money completely lost its value with the result that wage payments in kind were introduced. Labour was compulsorily mobilized; reward was defined in terms of social obligation: 'He who does not work, neither shall he eat.' Ration books of several categories were introduced and related to labour performed (Bergson, 1944), and the real income differential between skilled and unskilled and between manual and non-manual labour narrowed. In the early months of 1917, earnings of the most skilled workers were 232 per cent of the unskilled labourers, whereas by 1921 they had fallen to 102 per cent. At this latter date, wages in kind came to some 94 per cent of total income, and those in money only to about 6 per cent.[8] This period (1919–21) was one of egalitarianism. But the Communists had to face up to the problem posed by the division of labour – should workers in short supply, with higher skills and qualifications receive more of the economic surplus than their fellow workers? The short-term answer the Communists adopted was that differentials were necessary, but that they should be as small as possible. The immediate post-revolutionary period was one of emergency, geared to the need to maintain the Communists in power and to distribute resources to keep people alive and no new practical principles of wages and labour were introduced.

With the abolition of payment in kind in 1921, wages in practice were fixed through the market – by bargaining between workers and employers. The revival of market relations generally, therefore, led to prices and wages being determined by the forces of supply and demand in much the same fashion as in pre-revolutionary Russia.[9] While the trade unions fixed minimum wages rates[10] which reduced differentials much below

8. Figures calculated by Strumilin, cited by Baykov (1947, p. 43).

9. The Soviet economist Kostin cites figures which show that wage rates in pre-revolutionary Russia were similar to those of Russia in 1925–6 (1960, p. 16).

10. The wage structure had seventeen divisions covering all non-manual and manual workers: the greatest differential between skilled and unskilled manual workers was $3\frac{1}{2}$; the ratio of the highest basic salary to the lowest was 1:8 (Bergson, 1944, p. 185).

the pre-war levels, a comparative study by Bergson has shown that in fact earnings were similar in scale to those pertaining in the U S A in 1904 (1944, p. 92).

According to Soviet theory, egalitarianism would only be reached with full communism when all would receive 'according to their need'. In the early 1930s, Stalin emphasized that in the course of building socialism, workers could only be paid according to their work. He strongly opposed those who felt that under socialism wage differentials should be low:

Equalitarianism owes its origin to the individual peasant type of mentality, the psychology of share and share alike, the psychology of primitive 'communism'. Equalitarianism has nothing in common with Marxist socialism. Only people who are unacquainted with Marxism can have the primitive notion that the Russian Bolsheviks want to pool all wealth and then share it out equally. That is the notion of people who have nothing in common with Marxism (1955, pp. 120–21).

Consequently, much steeper differentials were introduced. In so far as earned income was concerned, in the U S S R a similar pattern of wage inequality has been evolved as in capitalist societies (Dewar, 1962, p. 80).

There is some confusion between the notion of class in a Marxist sense and the prevalence of wage inequality. The abolition of classes does not necessarily entail the elimination of wage inequality. This highlights a division between, on the one hand, the social policy of modern social-democratic politicians and Anarchists[11] whose philosophy is strongly tempered with beliefs about distributive justice and that, on the other, of Marxists who emphasize class, ownership and

11. For example, Crosland (1956) says: 'This belief in social equality, which has been the strongest ethical inspiration of virtually every socialist doctrine, still remains the most characteristic feature of socialist thought today' (p. 113). See also Jenkins (1952). For Anarchist thinkers, Kropotkin (1888, pp. 8–13) 'We consider that an equitable organization of society can only arise when every wage system is abandoned and when everyone contributing for the common well-being to the full extent of his capacities shall enjoy also from the common stock of society to the fullest possible extent of his needs' (p. 16). See also Woodcock (1962, p. 202).

political rights. Though Marx too saw communist society in its ultimate form as being without differential rewards.

Let us now sum up the principal characteristics of the early Soviet regime which are of relevance to this study. As Goldthorpe has suggested (1967, pp. 655–91), it is true that in a state-socialist society, the polity plays an important role in determining the class structure and the system of social stratification. The October Revolution destroyed some social groups (the aristocracy, large-scale private farmers, shopkeepers, financiers, the retainers on the large estates), decisively strengthened the working class and secured the formation of other groups (collective farmers, commissars, the 'Soviet intelligentsia'). This was the work of a political elite. But one must not naïvely think that in this process Soviet Communists designed a social structure in keeping with a political ideology. To quote from Marx, they made their own history not as they pleased, but 'under circumstances directly encountered, given and transmitted from the past'. The norms and values of different groups in the society set limits to the policies the political elites could enforce. For example, at a very early stage after the Revolution, the expectations of skilled workers for higher remuneration were recognized and later, during the industrialization process, the need for incentives to encourage workers into skilled and responsible jobs and to maintain a stable factory work-force resulted in even steeper wage differentials. But we can hardly infer from the early history of Soviet Russia that socialism is impracticable or utopian. Even less can this evidence be used to refute Marx's notion of an egalitarian communist form of social organization. The reasons are clear. First, the economic basis inherited from Tsarist Russia had only just outgrown feudalism. Rather than introducing a socialist society qualitatively superior to capitalism, the Soviet regime in practice was faced with the construction of a technological basis similar to that of capitalist societies and it would be utopian to imagine that a socialist form of social relations could be constructed on it. Secondly, according to Marx, equality could only be achieved, and the dignity of manual labour ensured, when the division of labour was no longer necessary, when the material resources of production made such divisions no longer a requisite of the needs of industrial production. The structure of Soviet Russia in no way fulfilled this condition. The Russian Communists adapted Marxism to Soviet conditions. For Marx the 'dictatorship of the proletariat' was to be a relatively short period of rule, during which the working class (the majority) would preserve a social order superior to capitalism. In the Soviet Union the 'dictatorship of the proletariat' was an era of quite a different kind. The notion was utilized to justify the rule of the Communist Party which at best represented only the proletarian minority of the population. The party used its power to transform the country, to carry out industrial growth, to introduce large-scale agriculture in the countryside. The policies had important effects on the structure of the population, they facilitated the growth of the working class and the movement of the population to the town. But rather than the consolidation of the rule of the proletariat as envisaged by Marx, the 'dictatorship of the proletariat' made the conditions in which a proletariat was created.

State socialism

At the beginning of this chapter, we noted four main historical phases in the history of Soviet society. Above we have seen what happened in the area of social stratification in the first two – the period of social revolution and the years of industrialization. In this section we may now turn to the third phase, that of the building of socialism.

For Marx, the 'dictatorship of the proletariat' was to be a short transitory period between the capitalist and communist epochs. In the Soviet Union, the 'dictatorship of the proletariat' lasted nineteen years, from 1917 to 1936. In the latter year the USSR was *officially* defined as a 'socialist' society:[12]

12. In the states of Eastern Europe the pattern was similar but not identical. The first official classification was that of a 'people's democracy'. This was a political order based on an alliance between several classes: there was no dominant class or ruling party – in theory. The dictatorship of the proletariat was proclaimed in the second stage. The third stage was the socialist which usually is considered to be the social

the first stage of the October Revolution, the dictatorship of the proletariat, had been consolidated. The previous ruling classes, it was argued, had been destroyed and the industrial basis of the USSR had been laid. Stalin believed that the economic changes which had taken place between 1924 and 1936 had 'destroyed and liquidated the exploitation of man by man', and had entailed the 'liquidation of all exploiting classes' (1967, pp. 141–2). He triumphantly declared that 'in principle, the first phase of communism, socialism, has been realized' (p. 149). In Soviet Marxist terms, it was argued that there was a complete correspondence between the productive relations and the character of forces of production in Soviet society. If we interpret Marxist theory literally as Stalin did, after 1936 there could be no antagonistic 'classes' in the USSR for social classes are formed on the basis of ownership relations. As private ownership of the means of production had been progressively eliminated, so too had been the property owning classes, and since political power was held to derive from ownership, it followed that there could be no ruling and exploited classes. Socialist society, as defined by Stalin, was a harmonious society based on comradely cooperation.

The economic foundation of the USSR is the socialist system of economy and the socialist ownership of the instruments and means of production firmly established as a result of the abolition of the capitalist system of economy, private ownership of the instruments and means of production, and the exploitation of man by man (Constitution of the USSR, article 4).

Let us leave aside until later criticisms of this view, which may be provided by alternative analyses of Soviet reality, in order to discuss for a moment the 'official' description of the social structure since 1936. This may be regarded as the transformation of Marxism into an ideology which justifies the rights of the Communist rulers, and seeks to make legitimate

form of a society with a large proportion of nationalized industry and trade and particularly collectivized agriculture. It is important, however, to note that only Czechoslovakia (in 1960) and Yugoslavia (in 1963) have constitutionally defined their societies to be 'socialist' (Skilling, 1966, ch. 5).

the social relations they created in Soviet Russia (see Lipset, 1969, pp. 208–9). As in original Marxism, social relations are regarded as being determined by class relations; and in Stalin's Russia there were the working class and the peasantry, and one social stratum: the intelligentsia. The Soviet *working class* was no longer a proletariat, because it was not exploited by a ruling class. On the contrary, on the basis of socialist property, it helped guide Soviet society to communism (Stalin, 1967, pp. 142–3). By the Soviet *peasantry*, Stalin referred to farmers engaged in agricultural production on collective farms. They were distinguished as a class from workers because they were in *cooperative* production. Though the land had been nationalized, they collectively owned its produce and the seeds used for production:

In the collective farm, although the means of production (land, machines) do belong to the state, the product of production is the property of different collective farms, since the labour as well as the seed, is their own, while the land, which has been turned over to the collective farms in perpetual tenure, is used by them as their own property, in spite of the fact that they cannot sell, lease or mortgage it (Stalin, 1952, p. 19).

The essential class difference between the workers and collective farm peasants was one of ownership relations. Even though they did not own the large-scale machinery which was then kept under state control in machine tractor stations, the peasants still had collective ownership over at least part of the means of production. The working class, on the other hand, was employed in nationalized state-run enterprises and their work was planned, regulated and defined by the government, whereas these aspects of labour in the collective farm were under the jurisdiction of the general farm meeting.

In addition to the two classes described above, there was also the *intelligentsia* which was a stratum technically part of the working class and composed of non-manual rather than manual workers. Stalin included in this category a wide range of employees – engineering and technical, those 'on the cultural front' and 'workers by brain (*sluzhashchie*) in general' (1967, p. 145). This stratum embraced those in the strategic commanding and creative roles in society, as well as the more menial clerical and administrative jobs. The chief distinction between manual workers and the intelligentsia then is based on the role each group plays in the social organization of labour.

These two classes and one stratum have, in Soviet theory, a common interest, together 'in one harness' they carry out 'the building of a new classless socialist society'. From a knowledge of Marxist theory, one might expect that social change would continue until a classless society had been achieved. Stalin indeed said that the distance between these social groups would be reduced more and more (1967, p. 146). Here, however, we have a problem: in Marxist theory, change is the result of a dialectical process, it is a synthesis of thesis and antithesis. But how could one have a dialectical synthesis in a society characterized by social harmony, in which all antagonistic class contradictions had been resolved? Stalin did not face up to this problem when he discussed the class structure of Soviet society in 1936, though he noted that the 'economic . . . and political contradictions between these social groups will recede and will wipe themselves out'. Later attempts during Stalin's lifetime to discuss the problem of contradictions were not very penetrating. The view generally held was that put forward in a leading article in *Pod znamenem marksizma*: 'the complete harmony between the forces of production and production relations of socialism does not presuppose, but *excludes* contradictions between them' (Shtraks, 1966, pp. 32–3).

Non-antagonistic and antagonistic contradictions

There are two theoretical attempts to resolve the problem just described. The first is that adopted by anti-Soviet Marxists. They consider that the class struggle and irreconcilable contradictions persist in the USSR. We shall postpone our discussion of these views until later (see pp. 41–4). A second explanation is that favoured by Soviet Marxists themselves: 'non-antagonistic' contradictions, they say, will persist in Soviet society until the final stage, communist society, is reached.

The latter thesis involves a distinction between a non-antagonistic and an antagonistic contradiction. A non-antagonistic contradiction is one which may be resolved by quantitative change, whereas an antagonistic contradiction can only be resolved by a qualitative one. In the first case a contradiction may be resolved *within the parameters* of a given social system, in the second case, the nature of the social system itself must be changed (Shtraks, 1966, pp. 32–3). A non-antagonistic contradiction would involve adjustments between groups or institutions whereas an antagonistic one could only be resolved by the formation of a new social order (capitalism, communism).

Another way to look at the problem is to consider the relation between basis and superstructure. The *basis* is composed of two elements: the forces of production (tools and technology) and production relations (property relations). In a state-socialist society the relationship between these two elements of the basis is a harmonious one whereas in capitalist society such relations are antagonistic – the capitalist property relations are a fetter on the development of the forces of production. The *superstructure* is a set of institutions (educational, religious, political, social) which are functionally linked to the basis. Thus, it is argued, the sources of 'non-antagonistic' contradictions in state-socialist society may be found either in the basis due to the persistence of pre-socialist technological forms, or in a possible incongruity between basis and superstructure, for example administrative institutions (such as the regional economic councils) may be inappropriate to the productive forces or there may be 'remnants' of bourgeois ideology – religion, nationality (Shtraks, 1966, pp. 77–8).

In my view, it is confusing and inappropriate to use the term 'non-antagonistic contradiction'. The definition of 'contradiction' involves the antagonism of thesis and antithesis, and its resolution by a qualitative change in which the opposing elements find their synthesis at a new and higher level. The dialectic entails a process which is self-sustaining. But in the official Soviet theory, set out above, we have no such opposition, resolution and synthesis. As a social process, 'non-antagonistic contradictions' are externally regulated by the political system, and would more appropriately be referred to as 'incongruencies' or 'dysfunctions'. From the viewpoint of the official model, one might say that in Soviet society, certain values, groups and practices are at variance with the central value system and the dominant social, economic and political institutions: in other words, their existence is *dysfunctional* to the attainment of goals that are defined by the political elites. In Soviet terms these are either remnants from the old pre-socialist society or else they have an exogenous origin in the decadent capitalist order. Social change takes place, not by the resolution of internal contradictions involving qualitative leaps, such as that from capitalism to socialism, but rather by guided growth. As a Soviet writer says of the social structure: 'Under the conditions of socialism, where there is no state of class opposites, the remains of social inequality in significant part are connected with the character of labour and the cultural-technical level of the mass of workers' (*Problemy izmeneniya sotsial'noy struktury Sovetskogo obshchestve*, 1968, p. 61).

The same writer defines four main areas of social inequality. First, there are distinctions based on class relationships. Secondly, there are differences between rural and urban populations. Thirdly, distinctions persist between manual and non-manual labour. Finally, there are differences associated with various trades, skills and incomes (Glezerman, 1968). These four distinctions provide the basis for most Soviet sociologists' descriptions of social stratification in modern Russia (the epoch of the building of communism). But before examining them in more detail (chapter 3), it is necessary to discuss some alternative interpretations of the Soviet social structure.

2 Conflict Models of Classes in Soviet-Type Society

The views we have discussed so far constitute the official version of social reality: they emphasize consensus rather than conflict and hierarchy rather than dichotomy. It need hardly be said that other writers on the Soviet Union have strenuously attacked this image of social harmony and have argued that on the contrary the pattern of social relations is characterized by an opposition, sometimes manifest but more often latent, between conflicting groups. Such theories have in common the notion that inequality and stratification in Soviet society are in essence of a *political* nature. While these critics often disagree about the particular configuration of the ruling groups and about whether they are best described as classes or elites, they do agree that one social group rules over another and that the dominant group exploits the masses. In this chapter we shall consider theories which are the antithesis of the Soviet view and in chapter 5 we shall turn to examine the empirical data.

One type of conflict theory uses the terminology of class and is considered, by its protagonists at any rate, to be Marxian in orientation. A second type of theory defines conflict in terms of elite and mass and is explicitly anti-Marxist in its viewpoint. Like Marxism, these are theories of society which embrace many aspects of the social system in addition to social stratification. Here the main problem with which we shall be concerned is the nature of socio-political stratification in a system where, as Soviet Marxists maintain, private ownership of the means of production has been abolished.

The neo-Marxist class bureaucratic model

While there are many streams of thought represented by various Marxist groups, they share the same view of the cardinal features of the Soviet system of social stratification. Here I shall discuss Trotsky's theory and its development by Kuron and Modzelewski.

Trotsky accepted Marx's definition of classes as being 'characterized by their position in the social system of economy and primarily by their relation to the means of production' (1945, p. 248). He agreed that the class character of the Soviet Union was 'proletarian' – in so far as this had been guaranteed by 'the nationalization of the land, the means of industrial production, transport and exchange, together with the monopoly of foreign trade...'. But Trotsky denied that the interests of the proletariat were being served by the incumbents of political power. In particular, he distinguished between the interests of the proletariat and its political organization, the Communist Party, and the interests of those who were in the commanding positions of the bureaucracy. It was the bureaucracy, he argued, which had lodged itself in an exploitative relationship over the working class.

Arguing from Marxist theory, he held that under capitalism the bureaucrats who run the government and the capitalist corporations play a subservient role to the ruling property-owning classes. But in Soviet society the working class which was 'hardly emerging from destitution and darkness, [had] no tradition of domination or command' and therefore such a bureaucratic group was able to manipulate its position to become 'the sole privileged and commanding stratum in Soviet society' (1945, pp. 248–9). But although the polarization of socialist society was between this group and the working class, the dominant exploiting stratum was not a class in the Marxist sense for it had 'neither stocks nor bonds. It is recruited, supplemented and renewed in the manner of an administrative hierarchy, independently of any special property relations of its own [and] the individual bureaucrat cannot transmit to his heirs his rights in the exploitation of the state apparatus' (p. 249).

In Trotsky's view this privileged stratum did not have the characteristics of ruling classes in the classical Marxist sense. It sought to 'conceal its income' and in denying its own existence, it is 'equivocal and undignified'. Trotsky's theory does not assume that people are aware of the polarization of power and wealth. Here then we have a situation in which individuals may not be conscious of the way exploitation takes place. They are manipulated. They may *think* that they take the decisions even though effective power is denied them, or they may believe that society is based on equality whereas in fact they are exploited. However, Trotsky held that with its maturation, the working class would come to perceive the objective opposition of interests in the society and would overthrow the bureaucracy by revolution.

Trotsky and his followers do not accept the diachronic scheme put by Soviet Marxists, described above. Rather than a *progression* from the revolution through the dictatorship of the proletariat to socialism, they describe uneven change. The economic achievements of the USSR by 1936 are acknowledged:

Gigantic achievements in industry, enormously promising beginnings in agriculture, an extraordinary growth of the old industrial cities and building of new ones, a rapid increase of the number of workers, a rise in cultural level and cultural demands – such are the indubitable results of the October Revolution, in which the prophets of the old world tried to see the grave of human civilization. . . . Socialism has demonstrated its right to victory, not on the pages of *Das Kapital*, but in an industrial arena comprising a sixth part of the earth's surface – not in the language of dialectics, but in the language of steel, cement and electricity (Trotsky, 1945, p. 8).

Politically, however, they saw the Soviet Union as degenerating. Trotsky's supporters point out that from the time of the suppression of the Kronstadt revolt (1921) (though supported by Trotsky) democracy began to be undermined, it suffered a terrific blow when Trotsky's opposition to Stalin was defeated (1923) and when Trotsky himself was deported in 1929.

The purges of the 1930s were in Trotsky's view the culmination of despotism and Stalin's claim to have achieved socialism by 1936 was blatantly false. Socialism could not be reached in one country alone, especially in a backward society such as the USSR. For capitalism it was argued was supra-national in character and its contradictions would penetrate the Soviet Union to make impossible the development of society on a qualitatively higher (socialist) level. To achieve socialism Trotsky considered that a revolution was necessary in other advanced capitalist countries. Such a revolution would create the economic and political basis for socialism on a world scale.

Depending heavily on Trotsky's analysis, but extending it in some important respects, is the bureaucratic class model expounded by Rizzi (1939)' Djilas (1966), Schachtman (1962) and, more recently, by Kuron and Modzelewski (1968).[1] It is sometimes called a 'state capitalist' theory of societies of the Soviet type. Unlike the traditional Trotskyite theory which depicted a ruling *stratum*, this theory emphasizes the domination of a new bureaucratic *class* over the working class. It is argued that, whereas under private enterprise capitalism individual shareholders own the means of production, in societies organized on the Soviet model, it is the state which has the formal powers of ownership. But the state as a collective body is controlled by bureaucrats who have *de facto* control of the state.

History has seen examples of class and antagonistic societies in which state ownership of the means of production has prevailed (the so-called Asiatic method of production).

State ownership of the means of production is only a *form* of ownership. It is exercised by those social groups to which the state belongs. In a nationalized economic system, only those who participate in, or can influence, decisions of an economic nature (such as the means of production, the distribution of, and profiting from, the product) can affect the decisions of the state. Political power is concerned with power over the process of production and the distribution of the product (Kuron and Modzelewski, 1968, p. 6).

1. Rizzi (1939) is usually credited with the first 'state capitalist' explanation of the USSR. He was followed by Burnham (1941), and Cohn-Bendit (1969) has adopted a similar position (see p. 201).

This class, 'the central political bureaucracy' (p. 15), acts as a ruling class and like the bourgeoisie under capitalism, the economic surplus which it extracts from the workers gives it social and economic privileges. Moreover, it is able to justify its leading role by an adaptation of Marxism to an ideology of class consensus which serves to stupefy the working class.

Like Trotsky's view of Soviet development in the 1930s, Kuron and Modzelewski see the early phases of state-socialist industrialization in Poland as corresponding 'to the demands of economic development and the general interests of society' (p. 26). The achievements of the industrialization process, however, entailed the transformation of the political order into a 'class dictatorship by the bureaucracy'.

It may be said ... that the nature of the task of industrializing a backward country called to life as a ruling class a bureaucracy which was able to achieve this task, since it alone, through its class interest, represented the interest of industrialization under such conditions – production for the sake of production (p. 27).

In contrast to the Soviet theory considered in chapter 1, the bureaucratic model sees class rule being strengthened by industrialization and urbanization which provide the basis for the extraction of surplus by the bureaucratic class from the workers.

It seems to me that these theories, though deficient in some respects, illuminate many inadequacies in the 'official' Soviet theory. To begin with, the general point that *control* of the means of production rests in relatively few hands is well taken. The failure to acknowledge the possibility of political control being vested in a bureaucracy is a serious shortcoming of the Soviet theory and one that has had serious consequences for the Soviet political elite itself. For if there are no 'antagonistic contradictions' then it may be argued that there cannot be any need for a ruling political party to maintain the hegemony of one class (the working class). This was the basis of the justification of the forms of 'pluralism' which were introduced in Czechoslovakia by Dubček in 1968, when the 'guiding' role of the party was to be replaced by a more open and pluralistic political system.

However, since the Soviet intervention of Czechoslovakia, a theoretical justification of continuing party hegemony has been made. Glezerman (1968) has argued that classes are groups of people who can appropriate the labour of others due to the position they occupy in the economy. According to this theory, it might be possible for a particular stratum, say the cultural intelligentsia, to mislead the population by virtue of its control of communications. This tendency might originate in the bourgeois origins of such strata. Therefore, says Glezerman, the political arm of the working class, the party, must continue to safeguard the interests of the people and prevent a resurgence of capitalism and bourgeois nationalism. The Czech 'progressive' Communists, on the other hand, argued that there was a fundamental unity of interests between the intelligentsia and the working class, and that rather than the intelligentsia destroying the fabric of a socialist society it was the hegemony of the Communist Party that was an anachronism. Regardless of the truth of these two points of view, Glezerman has conceded that the *control* of a state-socialist society is a separate issue from ownership and that, as bureaucratic theorists have pointed out, groups in elite positions may not have the same interests as the workers. (In later chapters we shall consider social differences between them.) But bureaucratic critics, of course, would go much further and argue that the party elite itself is an exploiting class or stratum.

A second criticism of Soviet theory that is raised by the critics discussed above relates to the formal Marxist view of class. The point has already been made that in Marxist theory the relations of production are only one element which constitutes the basis of society, the level of technology being the other. Since the 'material forces' of Soviet (and other East European) society are not more highly developed than in the advanced capitalist countries, it is therefore open to question whether social relations can be at a higher level than those of capitalist countries, as the Marxist notion of a *socialist* system would have it.

Another disputable aspect of the Soviet theory is concerned with the notion of ownership. Ownership is a legal term defining the exclusive right of the individual to command over, dispose or enjoy the possessed object. Now the Soviet distinction between state and collective-farm property is a misleading one. For state ownership in fact does not convey equal rights to all citizens to enjoy and dispose of property. Government ministries and various organizations are given rights to the utilization of state property and these in turn give certain groups of individuals prerogatives which others do not have. Such rights are stringently enforced and give rise to the consciousness of property. Thus while one might concede that the Soviet state does indeed have the right to distribute property, the enjoyment of property is differentially distributed in state socialist society and the consciousness of property remains.[2]

The 'conflict theorists' described above are also open to serious criticism themselves. In the first place, Trotsky's theory is unclear about the constitution of 'bureaucracy'. It could be a horizontal grouping of incumbents of positions at the apex of the party, the ministries and the soviets (parliamentary organs). On the other hand, it could be a vertically integrated set of positions, such as the ministerial apparatus. If the bureaucracy is a horizontally integrated group, it would have to be shown that party secretaries and ministerial *nachal'niki* (heads) had an actual, rather than a possible or potential unity of interest, and that the pursuit of this interest involved the exploitation of the working class. If the 'bureaucracy' is made up of vertical ministerial institutions, it would have to be demonstrated that it could protect itself *against* the party and particularly against control by the party secretariat. Little empirical evidence has been collected to show the truth or falsity of these propositions.

It also seems doubtful whether the 'state-capitalist' theory succeeds in reconciling bureaucratic control with Marxist theory. Two main objections may be raised. First, the unity of

2. This would seem to modify the views of many theorists (such as Dahrendorf) who, arguing on the experience of state socialist societies, conclude that property as a form of inequality has been exaggerated. See 'On the origin of inequality among men', in Beteille (1969, p. 24). Dahrendorf is clearly wrong in thinking that property has little relevance in the USSR.

the bureaucratic groups again is not adequately demonstrated. According to Schachtman, the new ruling class includes managers and party secretaries at the factory level whose interests have become fused together in a way 'similar though not quite identical with historic fusings into one class of different social strata' (1962, p. 71). However, the decisions over production may be taken at a much higher level than the factory, and it is not at all obvious that the economic interests of factory managers and the political interests of political chiefs of party and government are necessarily congruent. Again if the theory is based on the assumption of the merging of interests of owners (party) and managers (the state administration), then this too must be demonstrated. While Schachtman's paper 'Russia's new ruling class' was originally published in 1942, it refers to the conditions of the 1930s. But at that time, as well as in the present, party and state administrations have been separate. Indeed, Djilas's 'new class' theory sees the party as the incumbent institution of class rule: 'The new ownership is not the same as the political government, but is created and aided by that government. The use, enjoyment and distribution of property is the privilege of the party and the party's top men' (1966, p. 65).

A second objection to state-capitalist theory which might be made concerns the notion of an ownership nexus between state property and the bureaucracy. However much *control* they have over Soviet production enterprises, managers and administrators can neither dispose of their assets for their private good, nor can their children have any exclusive rights to nationalized property. Kuron and Modzelewski avoid this issue by a 'party elite' explanation: the party elite is 'at one and the same time also the power elite; all decisions relating to state power are made by it ... by exercising state power, the party elite has at its disposal all the nationalized means of production ...' (1968, p. 7). They assume that the party and state are fused[3] and thus ignore the conflict that takes place

---

3. But allegiance to state or party institutions may be less acute in Poland than in the U S S R where structural differentiation has progressed much further.

between these groupings. Their argument that property is owned collectively by the bureaucracy cannot account satisfactorily for change and conflict within the system such as was demonstrated by the course of events in 1956 and 1970–71 in Poland or in 1968 in Czechoslovakia, which reflected the rise and fall of distinct groups *within* the (unitary) 'central political bureaucracy'.

These theories, stemming from a Marxist origin, emphasize objective class position: the incumbents of certain positions have rights and power which confer economic, social and political privileges even though the leading members of the bureaucracy may not be conscious of their class position. Djilas says that the new class is 'the least deluded and least conscious of itself' and that the communist 'is not conscious of the fact that he belongs to a new class, for he does not take into account the special privileges he enjoys. . . . He cannot see that . . . he belongs to a special social category: *the ownership class*' (1966, pp. 64–5). Conversely, the exploited may not necessarily be aware of the rulers' 'ownership' privileges, although writers such as Djilas take the view that at some stage a revolution will be necessary to overthrow the new class. Here again we encounter a difficulty: how and in what circumstances could a revolutionary working class arise? Trotsky himself saw a possibility that the party 'enriched with the attributes of old Bolshevism' itself might overthrow the bureaucracy and would restore democracy in the unions and freedom to political parties (1945, p. 252). But to advocate both Bolshevism and the freedom of political parties is to try to reconcile mutually exclusive ideas. None of the theorists of the 'bureaucratic class' mentioned solves this problem although some contemporary exponents of the state-capitalist theory do not look to the Leninist form of party organization as a means of regeneration but rather place their hopes on initiative coming from workers' control at the lowest levels. Cliff, for instance, sees the events of the Hungarian revolution as 'the great rehearsal' for such a revolution.

The workers spontaneously created a system of workers' councils which became the leaders of the entire people in revolt. These workers' councils which sprang up in different parts of the country immediately faced the task of federating. They were groping towards the establishment of a Soviet Republic (1964, p. 347).[4]

But there is very little evidence to suggest that the working class as such has developed a consciousness let alone any political organization which would form a basis for revolt against the ruling classes in the socialist societies we are considering. In Hungary in 1956, the liberation movement had a national rather than a class character. In Czechoslovakia, it will be remembered, the liberal measures of 1968 were introduced by the Communist Party and though they would have weakened party control over the ministries and ministerial control over industrial enterprises, they would have strengthened, rather than weakened, the power of managers. Indeed, the Soviet criticism of the intended changes in the Czech power structure was precisely that the party would lose control over the managerial social strata. From the greater freedom and initiative of industrial managers and the destruction of the central apparatus of central planning in favour of the market it was feared that a way would be paved for a free enterprise economy not unlike that in Western Europe. According to this viewpoint, workers' councils would not be effective mechanisms of control because the market would largely determine production and distribution policy, and workers' delegates to the councils would at best be able only to gain for the rank and file a greater share in the economic surplus of the firm. This in turn might have the undesirable effect of giving them a shareholders' mentality. It might be conceded that the faith which is placed by some theorists on reform 'from below' would at present appear to be neither politically nor socially realistic.[5]

The third and final criticism which may be levelled at the bureaucratic collectivist and the state-capitalist theories is that even if one can show that a particular social stratum takes

4. See also the detailed proposals for workers' control and workers' political parties in Kuron and Modzelewski (1968, pp. 59–68).

5. See also Riddell's criticisms of workers' control in Yugoslavia (1968, p. 58).

effective decisions over the means of production, it does not necessarily follow that the incumbents are acting in their own 'selfish' interests to exploit the masses. It is possible that other social forces play an important role in the decisions of the leadership. The bureaucracy is subject to rules or laws and the broader values and beliefs which give the system its legitimacy constitute a framework within which the elite must operate. Here the idea of the economic plan, and the notion of the building of communism are integrative mechanisms which bind the elites as much as the non-elites. The internal growth of Soviet society and its dynamism are the result of particular values which have set limits on the monopolization of power by the political elites.

The totalitarian-mass model

While the ruling and/or bureaucratic class theory has been accepted by many Marxists outside the official Communist Parties and by many ex-Marxists, yet another conflict theory has wide currency – that of totalitarianism. Like Marxism the totalitarian model is not simply confined to the study of social class and stratification, but sets out to show how the domination of the political system over society takes place after communist or fascist types of political parties have seized power.[6] In the present context we may define the social structure of totalitarian society as consisting basically of a dichotomous set of social relations between ruling elite and an amorphous, socially ineffective mass.

The best-known sociological discussions of totalitarianism are those of Kornhauser (1960), Aron (1950) and Arendt (1958). Aron's argument is quite ingenious. He attempts to combine Marx's class analysis and Pareto's elite theory. He concludes that a classless society is achieved under totali-

6. Friedrich and Brzezinski (1966, pp. 22–3) identify eight traits of a totalitarian system. The six main characteristics are: an official ideology, a single mass party typically led by one man, a system of terroristic policy control, a technologically conditioned near monopoly of control of the effective mass media and means of armed combat, central control and direction of the entire economy; two other, though less important, traits are also suggested: administrative control of justice and expansion.

tarianism; but unlike the kind of classless society envisaged by Marx, it is one in which an elite rules a fragmented mass. The unitary elite is made up of a

small number of men who in practice run the industrial undertakings, command the army, decide what proportion of the national resources should be allocated to savings and investment and fix scales of remuneration. This minority has infinitely more power than the political rulers in a democratic society, because both political and economic power are concentrated in their hands. . . . The unified elite has absolute and unbounded power. . . . A classless society leaves the mass of the population without any possible means of defence against the elite (1950, pt 2, p. 131).

Totalitarianism, argues Aron, solves the problem of conflict in modern society by reducing society to 'obedience' rather than, as Marx suggested, by general liberation. The elite must be monistic because otherwise all economic and political power will not be concentrated at one source which is a necessary condition for planning in a collectivized economy. Aron accepts the view that Soviet society is classless in Marxist terms: 'every member of the population has his share in ownership, since the means of production belong to the community, and everyone is a wage-earner because all incomes are derived from work'. Conflict between groups is abolished because of the strength of the unitary elite and the weakness of group cohesion among the masses.

The nature of totalitarian society has been described in detail by Arendt who holds that, unlike a society characterized by a hierarchical ranking of strata or even by a polarized system of classes, a mass society is composed of individuals who lack consciousness of common interest and who therefore cannot be integrated into interest groups. Arendt argues that, in Soviet society, Stalin 'fabricated an atomized and structureless mass' (1958, pp. 318–23; see also Feldmesser, 1966, p. 533). It follows from the theory of 'mass society' that a characteristic of a totalitarian social structure is its *lack* of structure which is deliberately promoted by the ruling elite. Arendt's view is that in Soviet Russia, group formations among the non-elites had to be abolished, otherwise they would have developed interests hostile to the ruling elite. The structure of intermediate groups in totalitarian theory has been somewhat refined by Kornhauser, who argues that not only are the intermediate groups weak, but that they are also 'inclusive', that is, controlled by the ruling elite through 'front' organizations. The ruling elite itself is made up of the top echelons of the party which has developed channels of direct access to the otherwise unorganized individuals in the society. Thus a state-socialist society is mainly distinguished from a modern capitalist one by the fact that in the former a unified political ruling elite determines the shape of the social system whereas in the latter there exists a number of competing elites who represent autonomous social groupings with different interests.

Most of the serious analyses of totalitarianism have been carried out by political scientists rather than sociologists,[7] and in general they have been concerned to define the structure of the ruling elite. Recent thinking has tended to question the idea of the monistic nature of the elite by showing that at the apex of power a number of specific interests may impinge upon the ruling apparatus (Meyer, 1964; Skilling and Griffiths, 1971). Meyer, for example, cites the interests of such groups as industrial and administrative executives, military and security officers, leading scientists and other highly placed opinion makers. This line of thought is an attempt to account for conflict within the ruling elite while at the same time preserving the basic conception of its unity against the non-elite, the mass. Meyer also considers the role played by social mobility in providing the recruitment of 'new blood' into the elite from the mass. This process not only helps to prevent the formation of a group consciousness among the subordinate population but gives some credence to a value system which is based on notions of merit and achievement.

It would take us outside the bounds of this text to discuss in detail the deficiencies of the totalitarian model, but some of the more important defects may be noted here. First, as we

7. See for example, Friedrich and Brzezinski (1966). This book is devoted to the analysis of the socio-political system rather than to inequality and social stratification as such.

saw above when criticizing the neo-Marxist theories, insufficient attention is given to the ideology which helps determine the path which social change should take. As was pointed out in chapter 1, terror was utilized by the Bolsheviks in the early period of Soviet rule against the *class* enemies of the regime and industrialization was not simply a policy adopted by the elites to help 'massify' the population, but was a policy in keeping with the development of society as postulated by historical materialism.

Second, it seems most unlikely that any society can remain in a state of perpetual terror or 'massification'. Personal security, the fulfilment of certain minimum expectations about one's career, living standards and the education of one's children would seem to be a minimum condition of social life in modern society. Also, the totalitarian model is an 'immanent' or static analysis ignoring changes in the structure of society through time. The point need not be laboured again that in state-socialist society urbanization and industrialization have had important consequences for the occupational and social structure. In the advanced phase of the development of these societies, professional and regional interests are articulated and play an important part in the political process.[8] The totalitarian model may be more appropriate to the period of rapid socialist industrialization than to the more mature industrial society. Totalitarianism stresses the coercive role of political elites, the importance of their control of mass communications and the means of violence while also giving a prominent place to the rapid social mobility and the purges of the 1930s. Applied to the present day, it is less useful. State-socialist societies are socially hierarchical and stratified. In the next chapters we shall study the extent of this inequality and privilege and we shall see that the dichotomy between a political elite and a mass society is an over-simplification of social reality.

8. I have ascribed elsewhere the role of different groups in the Soviet political process (Lane, 1970, chapter 8; see also Skilling and Griffiths, 1971).

3 Social Inequality: Soviet Sociology's Interpretation of the Social Structure

At the beginning of chapter 1, we noted four main historical phases in the history of Soviet society. Above we saw what happened in the area of social stratification during the first three – the period of social revolution, the years of industrialization and the first phase of the 'building of socialism'. The Stalinist, Trotskyite and totalitarian theories[1] derive from the experience of Stalin's Russia, particularly the decade of the 1930s and they have been concerned with political power in a society where property classes as known in capitalist societies have been destroyed. In this chapter we shall focus on what Soviet philosophers and sociologists call the period of the building of communism (the post-1956 period) and we shall be more concerned with description than theory. But it is important to note here that 'the facts' about societies have not been collected independently of the ways in which sociologists and others conceive (or desire) society to be arranged. In describing and explaining social stratification sociologists are often influenced by ideologies of social stratification. Established political elites encourage the propagation of views which justify their own power and the existing state of inequality, whereas revolutionaries express quite opposite convictions. Furthermore, a ruling party or political elite may not only legitimate its power by reference to a theory of society justifying inequality but it may direct research into socially (and politically) 'legitimate' topics and consequently in such societies it is sometimes impossible to investigate certain 'unauthorized' topics in the fields of class, power, social inequality or social relations. Theorists who emphasize class or group conflict are therefore at a considerable disadvantage in

1. That of Kuron and Modzelewski is excluded here.

the ideological struggle over defining the nature of Soviet society, because Soviet sociologists, when providing empirical data tend to select facts which do not vitiate the 'official' ideology of social harmony. Hence, in the chapters following this one, Soviet research will be supplemented by work carried out by non-Soviet sociologists.

The main characteristic of Soviet research into social stratification in Soviet society is that while inequality as such is studied it is denied that such inequality gives rise to social deference. By 'inequality' we mean that certain commodities or values, such as income, consumer goods and education are unequally distributed among groups of the population. Such groups may be described as being more or less privileged or under-privileged. But as Soviet sociologists point out, it does not follow that deference of prestige is correlated with inequality. Persons may, for example, have very unequal incomes but their respect for each other and the deference of third parties to them may be quite unrelated to income. As the hierarchical arrangement or ranking of individuals, groups and strata according to superiority and inferiority is alien to the Soviet conception of social relations under socialism, research into these topics is not pursued in the USSR. For the time being therefore we shall concentrate on the main kinds of inequality which Soviet sociologists have studied, which may be summarized under the four headings noted in chapter 1: inequalities between the collective-farm peasantry and the working class, between town and country, between manual and non-manual labour, and finally those arising from the division of labour which transcends the groups of worker, intelligentsia and peasant.

The working class and collective-farm peasantry

The working class is given pride of place in the Soviet sociologist's description of the Soviet social structure. It is 'the creator, the builder of a new society of labour'. It has as its aim the 'liquidation of class differences, the creation of a classless communist society' (Semenov, 1968, p. 6). The 'working class' which is divided into manual and non-manual workers includes all manpower engaged in state and public institutions (Pod'yachich, 1961). In 1969, the working class comprised 78·4 per cent of the working population, the *collective*-farm peasantry 21·57 per cent and independent peasants and craftsmen 0·03 per cent (Tsertnal'noe statisticheskoe upravlenie, 1970, p. 30). The working class, it should be noted, includes those employed in agriculture in state, as distinct from collective, farms.[2] The Soviet working class, in Soviet ideology, is not 'superior' to the peasantry in the sense of being economically or socially privileged, it is at a socially more advanced stage by virtue of ownership relations and is destined to build a communist society.

Whereas 'the worker' is employed by the state and does not own or market any of his produce, the 'collective farmer' is engaged in cooperative production and his income is dependent on the produce which is farmed and marketed cooperatively by the collective farm to which the government has leased the land 'in perpetuity'.[3] The collective farmer on a collective farm may be contrasted with the agricultural worker on a state farm. The state farm is organized like a factory by a ministry which owns the tools and produce and which appoints the farm director. The workers on state farms receive regular wages,[4] they may be members of trade unions and they have the same rights to welfare services as men employed in other industries. Indeed, the state farm is conceived of by

2. In 1968, 29 per cent of the employed population was in agriculture and forestry (Tsentral'noe statisticheskoe upravlenie, 1969, p. 545).

3. All farmers (state and collective) have the right to farm an individual plot, the produce of which may be sold on the free agricultural market. This small-scale production perpetuates the more traditional peasant mode of production. While the total area cultivated is small, the share of the plots in total agricultural output in 1962 came to 26 per cent of the potatoes, 7 per cent of vegetables and 34 per cent of the eggs (Shmelev, 1965, pp. 29, 35).

4. Until 1966 collective farmers received wages depending on the number of their labour days and the income of the farm. Their pay was irregular – sometimes quarterly in arrears. This system is being changed, in some areas collective farmers have similar wage rates to workers in state farms. Similarly, social security used to be provided by payments from the farm's own funds – not state funds.

Soviet theorists as a kind of agricultural factory, in which work is more mechanized, educational and cultural standards are higher than on collective farms and the men employed regard themselves as 'workers' rather than as smallholders working cooperatively.

Both Soviet and Western commentators agree that the Soviet collective farmer is not like the peasant in other parts of the world. As a unit of production, the 'ideal-typical' peasant household takes decisions over planting and harvesting and it is mostly dependent for its subsistence on goods produced on its own land. It is not only an economic unit but also a system of authority and welfare. The peasant family is normally patriarchal and its functions include both the socialization of children and provision for the old and infirm. Perhaps most important of all, the 'typical peasant' is held to have a close attachment to the soil; for him husbandry is a way of life with its own primordial rhythm. The Soviet peasantry, however, differs in important respects from this pattern. The activity of the collective farm must be 'in conformity' with the general economic plan. The farm must provide foodstuffs and raw materials (flax, cotton, etc.) essential to the needs of the economy. Therefore, it is the collective farm rather than the peasant household as such which takes decisions about agricultural production; and the product mix and methods of the collective farm are in turn closely supervised by the Ministry of Agriculture. Furthermore, the collective-farm *household* does not collectively receive payment according to the work its members provide on the farm but rather the latter receive payments as *individuals*. This has an important effect on family structure because the peasant wife and the children of working age have separate and independent sources of income which militate against forms of patriarchal authority. Moreover, the organization of education by the state also has the effect of weakening the family's socialization role. But perhaps the most important factor in the life of the Soviet peasant is political: while all peasants face political demands or pressures from the wider society, which may take the form of claims for economic surplus (in goods or labour power), the

Soviet collective farm is penetrated by the political ruling class in the form of the Communist Party branch. This plays a most important part in the selection of the farm chairman who is formally elected by the members of the farm. Because production is in cooperative (not state) ownership the Soviet collective farmer is regarded from the Soviet viewpoint as not being fully emancipated from the fetters of the capitalist mode of production. He still needs to be led, as it were, along the path of communism by the working class. 'Without the aid of the progressive class of society (i.e. the working class), the peasantry by itself may not achieve communism and may not surmount the remains of past petty-bourgeois narrow-mindedness' (*Problemy izmeneniya sotsial'noy struktury Sovetskogo obshchestve*, 1968, p. 69).

However, *Soviet theory* does not envisage the liquidation of these differences between the working class and the peasantry through class struggle. Change is conceived of in essentially non-dialectic terms in the form of a 'drawing together' of the collective-farm peasantry and working class in the process of building communism. It is expected that changes in the 'material base of the village' will affect the character of collective-farm production and the social relations which rest upon it. In 1966, 9 per cent of collective farmers were engaged in technical and administrative jobs, 13 per cent in mechanical work and 78 per cent were unskilled manual labourers (*Klassy, sotsial'nye sloi i gruppy v SSSR*, 1968, pp. 85-6). This last group, according to Soviet sociologists, constitutes the collective-farm peasantry proper. Those in mechanical or administrative jobs with a higher level of education are held to have a different attitude to work than the labourers. And the growth in mechanization of the farms which is envisaged will affect the internal social structure of the collective farms in such a way that the first two of the above groups will grow in size and the last one will decline. A rise in the productivity of labour will also make possible the reduction of the farm work-force and the migration of the rural population to urban centres. All these developments will tend to make the structure of collective farms more and more like industrial enterprises.

Forms of joint production between collective farms and state enterprises are planned to speed up the division of labour and undermine the 'cooperative' mode of production. Through this process, the collective farm cooperative form of property will 'grow over' into communist property (p. 87). The conditions of labour will approximate those of the working class as regular monthly wages and the state provision of a wide range of social services (free meals, children's nurseries, social insurance) become more widespread.

Town and country

At first sight, the merging of the collective-farm peasantry with the working class would appear to entail the elimination of differences between farmer and industrial worker. In fact, town/country distinctions go much deeper than that between collective farmer and industrial worker. The low population density of rural Russia gives unequal facilities to the large number of people who live in the countryside.[5] Because the rural population is thinly spread, the provision of the same level of social and cultural services as in the town is not economically feasible and there has been a tendency to concentrate services in urban centres. The town thus becomes a cultural and social centre, housing communications, theatres, specialized shops, hospitals and the higher educational establishments on which the village becomes heavily dependent. The standard of living is also generally lower in the village than in the town. In 1961, the 40 per cent of the employed population that was engaged in industry, building, transport and communication, received 51·8 per cent of the national income whereas the share of the 37 per cent of the population employed in agriculture was only 21·2 per cent (Bolgov, 1962, p. 106).

Soviet sociologists have described inequalities between town and country in several different ways. First, in the villages, a much higher proportion of labour is occupied in manual work and conversely a lower proportion is in non-manual. These

5. In the 1970 census, 44 per cent of the population was still classified as rural (*Pravda*, 17 April 1971).

occupational differences may be illustrated by a survey which found that while in the town of Sverdlovsk only 43 per cent of the work force was engaged in manual labour, the figure in a village settlement was 70 per cent, in a state farm, 86 per cent and in a collective farm 88 per cent (*Klassy sotsial'nye sloi i gruppy*, 1968, p. 128). Secondly, in the countryside educational standards are lower and social services worse than in the town. In 1959, for every thousand people living in towns there were thirty-two with higher education, whereas in the villages the comparable figure was only 5·6 (Bolgov, 1962, p. 107). The numbers of people employed in various aspects of social and communal services in town and village are shown in Table 3, from which it may readily be seen that the countryside has only about half the amount of service provision as the urban centres. But we must bear in mind that urban areas provide services such as hospitalization and higher education for the villages as well as for their own inhabitants. Thirdly, there is more direct evidence of the cultural impoverishment of rural life. Table 4 (p. 61) distinguishes between collective farm, state farm, village settlement and town district, and shows the proportion of families who own radios and television sets, the

Table 3

Urban/Rural Differences: People Employed in Social and Communal Services (1959)

| | Per ten thousand inhabitants | |
	Town	Village
Total engaged in social communal services	1507	716
Education (*Prosveshchenie*)	260	186
Health	230	90
Children's educational institutions	40	13
Public catering and trade	410	108
Domestic and welfare services	160	29

Source: Manevich (1966, p. 40).

size of their personal libraries, and the number of their subscriptions to journals. By all three measures the cultural level of the town is clearly superior. We see that 59 per cent of town families had television, 25·7 per cent had a library with more than a hundred books and 36·5 per cent subscribed to more than three papers and journals. By comparison the figures for collective-farm families were much lower – 0, 0·3 per cent and 13·2 per cent respectively.

Table 4

Cultural Level of Urban and Rural Population (1963)

	Collective farm	State farm	Village settlement	Town district
Families surveyed N	371	836	1040	315
Percentage of families having:				
Radio relay points	48·0	35·8	11·0	20·7
Radio sets	34·8	43·9	73·0	78·1
Television sets			22·0	59·0
Personal libraries				
1–10 books	15·1	5·0	8·2	4·7
11–50	13·5	22·5	26·0	33·2
51–100	3·5	3·8	8·3	19·3
More than 100	0·3	2·7	5·4	25·7
Subscriptions to papers and journals				
1	28·0	29·2	39·0	19·6
2–3	38·3	33·8	31·0	33·2
More than 3	13·2	7·7	5·0	36·5

Source: *Klassy, sotsial'nye sloi i gruppy* (1968, p. 127).

It is of course the intention that the differences between town and country will be eliminated through the movement of society to full communism. It is Soviet policy that the standards in villages are to be brought up to those in the town: collective farms will merge with state farms; general educational and social facilities are to be improved; and farming will be less labour- and more capital-intensive, thereby levelling up the village occupational structure to that of the town. But at present considerable inequalities remain.

Manual and non-manual labour

According to the Marxist theory of *capitalist* society, the executive, administrative and superior technical personnel occupy a peculiar place in the system of class relations. While such strata do not by objective class-position form part of the ruling class (they do not necessarily own the means of production), they are closely identified with it. They serve the interests of capitalism and they are recruited from the bourgeoisie.

Under the conditions of capitalist society the role of the intelligentsia is ambivalent. On the one hand, being assistants of the bourgeoisie in the organization of production, of labour and of administration, part of the intelligentsia gives complete and active help to the bourgeoisie in the exploitation of the working class. For these services it receives a share of surplus value. On the other hand, a part of the intelligentsia, especially its lower ranks, is subjected to savage exploitation by the bourgeoisie (Manevich, 1966, pp. 53–4).

Soviet sociologists deny that any similar antagonistic relationship exists between manual workers and such executive and administrative strata in the USSR on the grounds that there is no private property and because 'a significant part of the intelligentsia (is made up) of men who started as workers and of the children of workers'. The differences between manual and non-manual strata are created fundamentally by the division of labour. Manual and non-manual workers perform different roles in the 'social organization of labour'; manual workers work with their hands and non-manual with their brains. 'Engineers and technicians are occupied in the administration of production, workers are engaged chiefly in executive labour' (Semenov, 1962, p. 249). The role of these strata in the production process results in inequalities between them in income and consumption, in their cultural and technical levels and in their standard of living (Senerov, 1962; Mil'tykbaev, 1965, p. 89). Soviet sociologists perceive social relations in objective rather than subjective terms, recognizing as significant the division of labour and differential levels of consumption but denying that the occupational structure gives rise to superior and inferior social statuses. Thus this view of social relations does not see ranking say by income or level of education, as accompanied by evaluation in terms of social worth.

The broad classification of non-manual employees, or brain-workers, may be broken down into a number of distinct groups differentiated according to character of work, level of income and standard of living. The total number of brain-workers in the USSR in 1965 was just over twenty-five million, and about half of this number constitutes the intelligentsia proper, which is made up of those possessing higher or secondary specialist education (12·1 millions). Within the category of intelligentsia come the leaders of government departments and enterprises (1·3 million in 1965), those engaged in higher education and culture (art, literature, the press) (726,000) and the largest group, the 'urban technical intelligentsia' which was over four million strong (Manevich, 1966, pp. 20–21). At the other end of the spectrum of the non-manual group performing more routine and less theoretically demanding work are clerks, draughtsmen and teachers in infant schools.

Manual workers are also differentiated by the level of skill on which their rates of pay are calculated, there being six or seven grades of pay in most industries. The bottom grades of lowly skilled manual and non-manual workers in fact have similar pay scales, though the non-manual worker has a higher level of education. Differences between various strata of the manual and non-manual working class have been delineated by the research of Shkaratan (1967) and this is summarized on Table 5 (pp. 64–5). Shkaratan divides the working class by occupation, education, wages, Party/*Komsomol* (Young Communist League) membership and participation in social work. The 'objective' differences are clearly shown on the table. Education ranges from 6·5 years to 14 years (groups 8 and 2), income from 83·6 roubles to 172·9 roubles (groups 7 and 1), party membership varies from 13·8 per cent to 60·8 per cent (groups 8 and 1), and participation from 35·1 per cent to 84·2 per cent. The pay of group 7 (non-manual workers), it may be noted, is lower than that of the manual group 8, though the level of education is higher. Also the educational level of group 3 is higher than that of the formally non-manual group 4, though the rankings of earnings is reversed.

Table 5

Some Aspects of the Social Structure of Leningrad Engineering Workers

Group of workers	Education (years)	Wages roubles (monthly)	Party/ Komsomol membership (%)	Partici- pation in social work (%)
1 Management (factory directors, shop superinten- dents)	13·6	172·9	60·8	84·2
2 Non-manual workers in highly qualified technical-scientific jobs (designers)	14·0	127·0	40·2	70·4
3 Qualified non- manual workers (technologists, bookkeepers)	12·5	109·8	42·8	82·4
4 Highly qualified workers in jobs with mental and manual functions (tool setters)	8·8	129·0	37·6	79·2

Group of workers	Education (years)	Wages roubles (monthly)	Party Komsomol membership (%)	Participation in social work (%)
5 Qualified workers of superior manual work (fitters, welders)	8·3	120·0	37·4	60·7
6 Qualified manual workers (machine-tool operators, press operators)	8·2	107·5	39·5	54·3
7 Non-manual workers of medium qualifications (inspection and office workers)	9·1	83·6	27·1	54·5
8 Unqualified manual workers	6·5	97·5	13·8	35·1

Source: Adapted from Shkaratan (1967).

Soviet writers then have a picture of three main groups (non-manuals, manual workers and peasants) each one being sub-divided into objective strata based mainly on skill and occupation. Inequalities between them, it is believed, will decrease with the development of the productive forces, and a more unitary structure will develop. Some of the arguments in support of the elimination of class boundaries have already been encountered above. First, it is argued that technical change will result in a greater demand for professional and highly skilled workers and that the proportion of manual or semi-skilled workers will decline. In support of this view it is shown that between 1932 and 1961 the number of manual workers increased 325 per cent, while the number of engineering-technical personnel rose by 516 per cent (Semenov, 1962, p. 262).[6] Secondly, say Soviet theorists, the general

6. This does not rule out, of course, a much greater absolute growth in the number of manual workers.

cultural and educational level of the population as a whole will increase. The position of all workers will improve and become more alike as more facilities such as education and consumer goods become available. The equalization of 'consumption' will progressively counterbalance the distinctions associated with different kinds of work. Finally, from the official Soviet viewpoint the significance of differences in income between strata will be eliminated, partly by the increasing provision of 'free goods' (meals and transport) for all citizens and partly by a reduction of wage differentials themselves (Sukharevski, 1968, p. 296). In support of these claims it is pointed out that between 1957 and 1968, the minimum wage doubled, whereas the average wage increased by 41 per cent. A general narrowing of basic pay differentials and a greater equalization of earnings have taken place. Whereas wages in industry have increased by 9 per cent (1956–61 compared to 1964–5), in agriculture they have increased by 20 per cent (p. 301).[7]

But such views should be regarded with caution. Even in 1971, a fifth of the population were still members of collective farms, and it will take a very long time for conditions in the countryside to approximate to those in the town. Moreover, as we shall see later on in this text, equal money incomes of social strata are by no means accompanied by identical 'consumption' patterns, either of commodities or of educational opportunities. Another criticism of the Soviet notion of *sblizhenie* (drawing together) is that it is not equivalent to the communist idea of the elimination of the distinction between manual and non-manual work. Soviet sociologists recognize that both physical and intellectual work will be necessary for a considerable time to come.

One way of bringing together manual and non-manual labour, which is sometimes suggested in the USSR, is participation in different kinds of work by the same individual. This viewpoint is based on Marx's prognostication that in *communist* society there would be no division of labour:

In communist society where nobody has one exclusive sphere of activity but each can become accomplished in any branch he

7. Wage levels are discussed in more detail on pp. 74–9.

wishes, society regulates the general production and thus makes it possible for me to do one thing today and another tomorrow, to hunt in the morning, fish in the afternoon, rear cattle in the evening, criticize after dinner, just as I have a mind, without ever becoming hunter, fisherman, shepherd or critic (Marx and Engels, 1965, p. 45).

In the Soviet Union this might be put into practice, as suggested by Elmeev and his colleagues, by a person being both an engineering fitter *and* teaching history at school (1965, p. 46).[8] A similar view has sometimes been taken in China where intellectuals have been dispatched to the countryside to try their hand at manual work. (There are also political factors involved in this case.) This practice if developed on a large scale would probably do much to bring together mental and manual labour but in the present conditions of state socialist society, it may seriously hinder the efficiency of production.

It is also sometimes suggested in the Soviet Union that social differences associated with occupations will be diminished with the development of automation. With the growing technical complexity of machinery and the work process it is said that workers will have to be trained in both manual and mental skills to perform a certain task. Hence from this viewpoint, the supervisor of an automated production line must understand say, electrical engineering, and be able to perform skilled manual tasks to keep his line going. He is both a manual and a non-manual worker and in this way manual and mental labour is merged. This process, it is argued, is accompanied by the gradual abolition of manual jobs (road sweepers, machine operators). But in my view this theory does not solve the distinctions which arise between different kinds of work. Not all occupations will be affected by automation and it is doubtful whether all jobs will in fact involve both mental and manual labour. For instance, what kind of manual work will be performed by a teacher of sociology? It is also possible that automation may create an even more specialized and stratified

8. Polytechnical education in which students have a scientific education and are taught to use their hands is also a means by which the dignity of manual labour may be enhanced. It is difficult for us to evaluate the practical effects of polytechnical education in the USSR (Charlton, 1968).

division of labour than before (Blumberg, 1968, pp. 53–64). It is probably to be expected that with the further development of industrial society, the general standards of education will rise as they have done in the past.[9] Again, the development of technology will mean that a higher proportion of the work force will be 'specialists' and some Soviet sociologists have considerable confidence that the general rise in educational standards will reduce the gap between manual and non-manual workers (Iovchuk, 1962). But in so far as this tendency is true, there is nothing especially 'communist' about it – it is also characteristic of advanced industrial capitalist societies.

Further difficulties arise over those posts which are concerned with control over production or over other men. In a modern complex industrial society someone must take decisions, and many persons become specialized in administration. Here Soviet theorists do not advocate workers' management or the abolition of conventional administration which would involve a process of genuine 'collective decision-making'. Rather they see opportunities for workers to participate in and 'to control'[10] the administration through commissions and voluntary organizations (such as trade unions). A more fundamental way in which 'directing roles' are to diminish is through the 'withering away' of the state, that is by an increase in the number of part-time and voluntary participants in the administrative apparatus. This means that the trade unions, for example, will take over greater responsibility for labour discipline, that the Communist Party will exercise influence in industrial problems and that the voluntary militia (*druzhiniki*) will maintain law and public order. In these processes the power of men in executive jobs may be reduced.

As evidence of their progress, Soviet sociologists point out that the number of leaders (*rukovoditeli*) in administration declined by 22 per cent between 1939 and 1959. But even if

9. In 1939 only 15 per cent of workers in machine tools and metal working had more than seven years education, by 1959, the comparable figure was 53·3 per cent (Elmeer, 1965, p. 61).

10. In the sense of 'to check' rather than to exercise rights of direction over.

this decrease is not explained by changes in the span of control – giving fewer men more power – there are still nearly 400,000 leaders in administration, and the number of directors of industrial enterprises has risen between the two dates by 126 per cent to reach a total of 955,000 in 1959 (*Klassy, sotsial'nye sloi i gruppy v SSSR*, 1968, p. 147). In addition, there are another third of a million managers of shops and over 100,000 school directors. These numbers illustrate that the USSR is far from being a society where the number of people who tell others what to do is on the decline.

In the light of the foregoing data presented on the *Soviet notion* of the construction of a classless society some critical comments are in order. It seems to me that the really significant difference in the system of social stratification compared to Western industrial societies is the absence of a private propertied class possessing great concentrations of wealth. Otherwise, the USSR is not dramatically unlike Western industrial societies. There is a system of inequality closely related to occupation. Workers who have skills requiring training and education and who are in short supply tend to receive a greater financial reward than those who have little or no skill. It would therefore seem to be true that the USSR is entering an epoch of classlessness only if one defines class in terms of private individual ownership of productive means. For the rising level of skill and education associated with advanced industrialization would appear to be creating a system of social inequality which, save for its ownership class component, is very similar to that of Western capitalist states. Literacy is universal and an increasingly large but relatively privileged part of the population is receiving higher education. The relative number of unskilled jobs is falling and that of highly skilled categories is rising but both groups are likely to persist in the near future. Finally, even though the wage differential previously enjoyed by 'white-collar' workers is gradually giving way to greater equality of income (see pp. 72–3), differential incomes are very much part of the Soviet social structure. Even in the Soviet view of the foreseeable future, it would appear that though social differences are planned to decline, the structure of social inequality is to remain.

In this chapter we have considered the Soviet view of the building of communism. The social differences which have been described might be considered rather superficial ones ignoring many dimensions of social stratification which are important in the eyes of non-Soviet sociologists. Are there any statuses to which individuals defer? Does sex or nationality provide the basis of social inequality? Are there strata within the Soviet system (such as groups of intellectuals) which dominate, rather than cooperate, with the others? In the next chapters we shall turn to consider these aspects of social stratification as well as other forms of inequality.

4 Social Inequality:
Hierarchy and Privilege

While Marxists hold that class or market position is the central determinant of the system of inequality and social stratification, many, probably most, modern sociologists view stratification as being multidimensional, market position being only one of these dimensions. The clearest and best known statement of this approach to stratification is that of Parsons: 'Social stratification is ... the differential ranking of the human individuals who compose a given social system and their treatment as superior and inferior relative to one another in certain socially important respects' (1954, p. 69). Parsons goes on to assert that differential ranking is a 'really fundamental phenomenon of social systems'. In this concept of stratification many social roles and activities may be the basis of evaluation. As Barber has put it:

What one's job is, how handsomely one dresses, how much one knows, how well one plays games, how good a friend one is, how one practises religion, all these and a multitude of other social roles and activities are potentially bases of evaluation that may be applied to the members of a society in order to determine their relative position in the system of stratification (1957, pp. 19–20).

In this chapter we shall describe some of the chief ways in which people are differentiated from each other. We shall consider the distribution of income, occupational prestige and the extent to which these and other bases of differentiation such as, for example, those of sex and ethnic origin, correlate with social stratification.

Income differentials

Income is taken by modern sociologists to be an important index of social standing though categories defined by income statistics in themselves may not correspond to social groups, to a style of life or to political privilege. Politicians, for instance, might have little popular prestige, a fairly high income, but supreme political power. Bearing this caveat in mind, income is nevertheless a most important determinant of a person's life chances. Also the distribution of income may indicate the way certain social groups apportion the social surplus of a society. Many egalitarian thinkers regard an equal distribution of income to be an essential characteristic of a just society. Others, however, argue that wage differences are necessary in modern society to reward achievement and innovation and to ensure that the most suitable persons are allocated to various roles. From this viewpoint, a hierarchy of styles of life, of differential income and consumption patterns provides a stimulus to achievement which is an integral part of the system of modern production.

We have seen that after 1917 the social hierarchy in Russia was severely disrupted and that wage differentials were reduced as part of this process but were then widened again under Stalin's regime. Since the 1950s differentials have again narrowed. Let us now consider how at the present time material rewards are distributed between various occupational groups.

Available Soviet statistics are not very comprehensive on this score. 'Average wages' for various groups of industries are published in the annual statistical handbook[1] and these data may be supplemented by other fragments of information on specific kinds of jobs. The official minimum wage since 1966 has been 60 roubles per month and the average money wage in 1968 was 112·6 roubles (these include manual and non-manual workers but exclude collective farmers). The ratio of the lowest wage to the average is 60:112·6 which is a relatively low figure when compared to Western countries. Data are also published for separate industries: in building the average wage in 1968 was 127·3 roubles; on state farms 92·1 roubles; in transport 116·6 roubles (sailors got 154·41); in

1. In this respect, of course, in Britain the differences between lower white-collar workers and manual workers have also been reduced (see Bain, 1970, pp. 64–7; Lockwood, 1958, p. 211).

communications 88 roubles; in education 102·8 roubles; in science 129·4 roubles; and in administration (offices of government, trade unions, etc.) 118 roubles (Tsentral'noe statisticheskoe upravlene, 1969, pp. 555–6). Other averages have been published which show changes in the differentials over time for certain social groups (see Table 6).

Table 6

Wages of manual and non-manual workers: 1940, 1960, 1966

	Roubles per month		
	1940	1960	1966
Manual workers	32·3	89·8	104·4
Engineering and technical workers	68·9	133·0	150·1
Non-manual workers (unqualified)	35·8	73·2	88·2

Source: *Trud v SSSR* (1968).

These figures show that between 1940 and 1966 the position of manual workers has improved considerably by comparison with the other two groups[2] and that there is now a small gap between them and unqualified non-manual workers. Of course, the lowest paid are still in the countryside. It has been estimated that in 1964, when state farmers received an average of 70·6 roubles a month, the average collective farmer had a wage income of only some 31 roubles (Karcz, 1966, pp. 395–6) (but if other income from selling produce as well as the value of the food consumed on the job is allowed for, the latter figure rises to 55 roubles).

These figures give averages for rather general groups but tell us little about the range of incomes. On the basis of a Soviet source which lists wage *rates* (not actual earnings) we see that in 1959 a top director could receive as much as thirteen times the wage of the lowest grade of worker (Kostin, 1960, pp. 17, 19, 60–61).[3] I understand that in 1969 the salary of a Soviet

2. For comparative statistics on other East European countries see United Nations (1967, pt 2, table 8–18).

3. In Poland in 1966 the average wage of manual workers was 2147 zloties per month and the upper limit for factory directors has been estimated at 14,000 zloties (Pasieczny, 1968, p. 161).

government minister was 1050 roubles per month (about nine times the average wage). In addition there are other non-monetary benefits such as cars, houses, holiday facilities and special shops; and taking such items into consideration, it has been asserted that the ratio between the income of a factory manager and a manual worker ranges from 25–30:1 (Bottomore, 1965, p. 47). Such wide differentials, however, have not been backed up by empirical data. An even greater degree of income inequality has been suggested by Mehnert who has stated that the top incomes in the Soviet Union have been about 80,000 roubles per month (Lenski, 1966, p. 27), and if this is true, such a salary would be three hundred times the minimum and a hundred times the average income at the time the calculation was made. But, as Lenski has pointed out, even these differentials are *much less* than in the USA, where the comparable ranges are 11,000:1 between the highest and lowest and 7000:1 between the highest and the average. It is also important to bear in mind the fact that structural unemployment does not exist under state socialism, and the moral and social degradation associated with it has been abolished. Such differences are substantial and they imply that rewards on the American level are not 'necessary' to the maintenance of a modern economy. They also illustrate the well substantiated fact that 'capitalism produces extremely rich people with a great deal of capital, and this is the most striking difference between [income distribution under communism and capitalism]' (Wiles and Markowski, 1971, p. 344).

While Soviet data on income distribution are not very adequate much better statistics are available for other Eastern European societies. In Poland, wage differentials have followed a similar general pattern through time as in the Soviet Union. This is not surprising, of course, for after the Second World War the USSR was used as a model for the state-socialist societies of Eastern Europe. In the immediate post-war period in Poland there occurred a reduction in the level of differentials compared to pre-war Poland. One calculation has shown that in 1937 non-manual workers received three times as much as manual workers whereas their advantage was only 9 per cent greater in 1960. Comparing the range of incomes (highest and lowest) Wesolowski (1966) estimates that this has fallen from 200:1 in pre-war Poland to 10:1 in the 1960s. The distribution of incomes between manual and non-manual workers in 1963 is shown in Table 7 below. While there are eight times as many manual workers as non-manual workers in the very lowest category, and one and half times as many non-manuals as manuals in the top group, it can be seen that the majority of each falls in the range of 1201–2500 zlotys. Of course, the *very high* incomes, well over 3000 zlotys which are not defined here in detail, are probably to be found among the highest non-manual strata.

Table 7

Polish Gross Monthly Earnings according to Wage Groups (1963)

Wage group (zlotys)	Manual (percentage)	Non-manual (percentage)
701–800	10·7	1·3 ⎫
801–1000	7·2	5·4 ⎪
1001–1200	8·7	9·1 ⎬ 59·2
1201–1500	15·6	17·1 ⎪
1501–2000	24·7	26·3 ⎭
2001–2500	15·9 ⎫	16·3
2501–3000	8·5 ⎬ 33·1	10·4
over 3000	8·7 ⎭	14·1

Source: Cited by Wesolowski (1966, p. 27).

We may confidently generalize that one of the results of the Soviet pattern of nationalization and industrialization is a considerable equalization of income and living conditions. This does not mean that wage levelling or *uravnilovka* has been accepted as equitable by all the groups in a state-socialist society; indeed as we shall see later (pp. 104–5), the opposite is the case. But it seems to be a general pattern in such societies that the period immediately following the nationalization of property and the seizure of political power is characterized by income equalization. Later, with the consolidation of power by the new elites, greater differentials are introduced. In the USSR Stalin by virtue of his administrative control implemented such changes, whereas in Eastern Europe it is the self-styled anti-Stalinists who have called for greater reliance on market mechanisms, financial incentives and the abolition of the 'damaging levelling of wages'.[4]

The extent of such differences may be illustrated by research carried out in Hungary which provides data on patterns of consumption as well as income (Hungarian Central Statistical Office, 1967).[5] The Hungarian research shows, not only that wage income is differentiated, but also that it is spent on different things thereby giving rise to differing 'styles of living'.

In the groups in a more advantageous situation, and especially with a higher education, there is a strong trend toward the realization of a way of life which they consider more cultured.... The total yearly expense of education and entertainment increases from 86 forints in the group of agricultural cooperative members to 486 forints in the group of leading officials, intellectuals.... At the same time, there is only a 60 per cent difference in the value of total consumption (p. 79).

The top group spent 3·5 times more than average on newspapers, 2·5 more on the cinema, 33 times more on books and eight times as much on going to the theatre. The authors point out that the better educated strata not only have a 'more cultural manner of life' but eat better kinds of food, spend more on holidays and utilize more household appliances (washing machines, refrigerators, etc.).

Those with more income and better education also have a greater variety of consumption goods, which 'in certain cases reflect the demand for goods which are symbols of the social position' (p. 80). Higher professional occupation groups con-

4. Many economists in Czechoslovakia, for example, have argued that wage equality has had a most deleterious effect on the development and growth of the economy (Müller, 1969, pp. 48–9; Sik, 1967, pp. 203–4; Machonin, 1969, p. 158).

5. A survey of 1500 households carried out in 1963.

sume 5·5 times more coffee than unskilled operatives. They eat less beans, cabbage and bread but more mushrooms, asparagus and rolls. The top group spends fifty-four forints per capita per annum on cosmetics, whereas the unskilled operatives only spend nineteen forints. On domestic help and laundry, the upper professional groups spend 164 forints, other non-manual eighty-three forints, skilled/semi-skilled twenty-nine forints, unskilled seventeen forints, and agricultural cooperative workers only four forints. As the sample excluded households with domestic help living in, the actual differences are even greater than shown (p. 81).

The higher social groups also made greater use of the social services. While the health service is free, medicine is not. Leading officials and intellectuals spent thirty-four forints per capita per annum on medicine, and other non-manual workers, thirty-seven forints: but such spending by skilled/semi-skilled workers fell to twenty-two forints and by agricultural cooperative workers to nineteen forints. Housing is also differentiated by social group: the higher the social status, the better the housing. Some of the chief results of the Hungarian survey are summarized in Table 8, p. 78. It suggests a highly *hierarchical* social structure with a remarkably high correlation between income, housing and cultural level. Research conducted in Poland and Czechoslovakia shows lower but positive correlations between income, prestige and education. A study of 3381 persons in Poland in 1965 and 1967 shows that the correlation between education and the prestige of occupations is 0·35, between income and prestige 0·36, and between education and income 0·40 (Slomczynski, 1970, p. 18). In Czechoslovakia, Safar and others, following field research involving 13,215 respondents, have shown that 'style of life' is highly correlated with income (0·45), complexity of work (0·54) and education (0·61) (1970, p. 18).

We may conclude that while the range of money incomes is narrowed by the political authorities, nevertheless social strata in state-socialist societies are distinguished by differences in income and consumption patterns which are related to the place occupied in the division of labour. Occupation

Table 8

Social Position, per Capita Income, Housing and
Cultural Indexes

Social strata by occupation of head of household	Per capita income index (average = 100)	Index of housing standards (a) (average = 100)	Index of cultural level (b) (average = 100)
	A	B	C
Higher professionals	151	149	193
Average level experts	125	133	153
Office clerks	117	128	147
Skilled workers	107	109	110
Trained workers	93	91	87
Unskilled workers	81	86	67
Agricultural manual workers	86	79	60

Source: Adapted from Ferge (1966).

(a) Based on size, conveniences and equipment of houses.
(b) Cultural level combines average level of education of family, books, newspapers, radio and TV.

Correlation coefficient Columns A/B 0·97
A/C 0·98
B/C 0·99

appears to give rise to not only various quantitative differences in consumption, but to qualitative ones as well which manifest themselves in variations in the style and manner of life. The hypothesis that the major 'break' in the stratification system of state-socialist societies lies between skilled and unskilled rather than, as in Western captialist societies between manual and non-manual must be treated with some scepticism (Parkin, 1971, p. 147).[6] While a reduction in differentials between non-manual and manual has taken place, this need not entail a

6. In Poland, non-manual workers have longer holidays, better sick benefits and better conditions for leave to look after sick dependents than do manual workers. See 'Socjalistyezny kodeks pracy', *Polityka*, 12 October 1968 (no. 41), also pp. 84–6.

'proletarianization' of the white-collar worker. As Goldthorpe and others have been at pains to point out in respect of the notion of the 'bourgeoisification' of the English proletariat, even a convergence of certain aspects of the life-situation of manual and non-manual workers has not led to the assimilation of the former by the latter (Goldthorpe, 1969, pp. 23–9).

The discussion so far suffers from many defects: the inequalities described are mostly quantitative and the categories used have been devised mainly for statistical and economic purposes. While these deficiencies do not make invalid the inequalities described, they limit the sociological inferences we may wish to make. We do not know, for example, whether these categories are socially meaningful. Are the members of different income groups conscious of being in a status hierarchy, of being a stratum with a distinctive social standing relative to other groups? It is possible that the kinds of inequality described do not flow over into the evaluation of men in the numerous roles they play. It is claimed by many Soviet sociologists that individuals may be differentiated by skill, income and sex, but that a system of social evaluation or honour does not follow from these inequalities. The values of Soviet society they say are those of fraternal equality and the leaders of the Communist Party and factory labourers may regard each other as 'comrades' (for a different interpretation see Ossowski, 1963, p. 190). Soviet sociological research does not investigate whether there is hierarchy, gradation and deference between groups of individuals; and therefore we shall have to utilize studies which have been completed in Western society and the more sociologically advanced societies of Eastern Europe.

Occupational, prestige and social groupings

The best data available on status hierarchy in Soviet society are to be found in a study by Western sociologists of the evaluation of occupational roles in industrial societies. This research considers the prestige given to occupations in the USSR in relation to similar studies in five other advanced countries. The sources of the Soviet data were interviews conducted with 2146 Soviet displaced persons after the Second World War. The similarities in prestige ratings between the countries were measured by correlation coefficients and the results affecting the USSR and other countries are shown below (Inkeles and Rossi, 1956, p. 332).

	Japan	United Kingdom	New Zealand	United States	Germany
USSR	0·74	0·83	0·83	0·90	0·90

Here we see a remarkable similarity between the rankings. The researchers also analysed the discrepancies in each nation's ratings which account for the absence of a unitary correlation. The discrepancies in ranking of occupations are shown on Table 9.

Table 9

Differences in Occupational Rankings in the USSR and Other Countries.

Rated higher in:	Japan	USA	UK	NZ
Rated lower in USSR	Factory manager Farmer	Scientist Farmer	Farmer	Farmer
Rated lower in:	Japan	USA	UK	NZ
Rated higher in USSR	Accountant	Engineer Worker	Worker	Worker

Source: Adapted from Inkeles and Rossi (1956, p. 334).

The table brings out the main differences in the ranking of occupations. From it we may fairly safely make two inferences. First, the lower ranking given to the 'farmer' in the USSR is probably explained both by the inferior status given to the *krestyanin* (peasant) in pre-revolutionary Russia and to his *de facto* under-privilege in Soviet Russia. Second, the relatively exalted position of 'the worker' in the Soviet Union is directly attributable to the value system of communism. In the view of its authors, the general implications of this research are that 'there is a relatively invariable hierarchy of prestige associated with the industrial system, even when it is placed in the context of larger social systems which are otherwise differentiated in important respects' (p. 339).

The Soviet data utilized above were based on respondents' views on the 'general desirability' of the occupations. This is not the same as 'popular regard', or personal safety or personal satisfaction. Rossi and Inkeles (1957), using the same respondents have analysed the ratings given to occupations in five dimensions: general desirability, material position, personal satisfaction, safety (from arrest), popular regard. The desirability of occupations was highly correlated to personal satisfaction ($+0·898$), and quite highly correlated to popular regard ($+0·525$). On the other hand, jobs held high in popular regard were low on material position ($-0·180$): hence a doctor who was ranked first in popular regard was seventh in material position. Material position and safety were very negatively correlated ($-0·818$): the 'safest' occupation was believed to be 'rank-and-file worker', but its material position was bottom but one; on the other hand, a factory manager was ranked second in material position but was at the bottom of the safety scale.

While the above study of Soviet refugees has contributed greatly to our knowledge of stratification in the Soviet Union it refers to a period before 1941 and unfortunately the study of status and occupational prestige has not been carried out in the Soviet Union. However, Polish sociologists who have a different sociological tradition and much more contact with West European and American sociology have replicated the research of Inkeles and Rossi. Sarapata has shown that the correlation between 'Western' and Polish prestige hierarchies is very high: Poland (Warsaw) and the USA $0·882$; Poland (Warsaw) and England $0·862$; Poland (Warsaw) and West Germany $0·879$ (1966, p. 41).

The statistics of both the above surveys must be carefully interpreted. In the first place, the rankings are restricted to comparable occupations, and some important categories, such as party secretary, are excluded from the cross-national calculations. Also the Polish data refer to the metropolis and not to the countryside where more traditional values may persist. Secondly, the 'rankings' may overlook significant differences in social distance and may be too gross in character to show up other socially significant variations. For instance, while the occupations of trained engineer and skilled worker may have similar 'ranks' in two societies, the relative degree of the 'desirability' of their jobs may be very different and the process of interaction between the groups is yet another distinct question.

Table 10

Comparable Rating of Occupational Groups in Poland and West Germany by Prestige

West Germany		Poland	
Occupational group	Rank	Occupational group	Rank
Capitalists, directors, high officials	1	Intelligentsia	1
Intelligentsia	2	Skilled workers	2
Mental workers A (bookkeeper, draughtsman)	3	Mental workers A	3
Small capitalists and handicraftsmen	4	Petty capitalists and handicraftsmen	4
Skilled workers	5	Mental workers B	5
Mental workers B (post-office clerk, insurance agent, salesman, conductor)	6	Unskilled labour	6
Semi-skilled workers	7		
Unskilled labour	8		

Source: Sarapata (1966, p. 43).

A second table constructed by Sarapata which compares occupational groups in West Germany and Poland attempts to bring out such differences (Table 10 above). Sarapata suggests that there is less of a hierarchy, that is possibly less social distance between the top and bottom occupations in Poland than in West Germany, though the different *number* of ranks shown (six and eight) may reflect the research design and may not prove very much about social distance. Perhaps the most important conclusion to be drawn from the table is the difference in values effected by the state ownership of industry. The prestige of strata based on economic-class position (such as capitalists, directors) and higher officials is of less significance in Poland than Germany. Table 11 (below) shows what people thought of the status of certain occupations in modern Poland as compared with their status in pre-war Poland. Workers using their hands, both skilled and unskilled, rose very much in popular esteem whereas non-manual groups (such as merchants and priests) suffered a decline. Thus the impact of nationalization, of the ideology of state socialism, cannot be dismissed as unimportant: it had a profound effect not only in changing the occupational structure but also on the prestige of some occupations. But the upper professional occupations stand out as being consistently high in desirability and popular regard in both periods. Those with the social

Table 11

Respondents' Evaluations of the Change in Status of Selected Occupations (in percentages)

Occupation	*As compared with the pre-war period the status of the occupation is now*		
	Higher	*The same*	*Lower*
Engineer	39	35	26
Locksmith working for wages	49	21	30
Miner coal-hewer	81	14	5
Unskilled building worker	68	21	11
White collar worker	24	32	44
Workshop owner	15	25	60
Merchant	9	25	66
Priest	8	25	67

Source: Sarapata (1966, p. 38).

function of control of life itself (physician), the understanding and control of nature (scientist and engineer) are almost always given wide social recognition and high prestige. There is no contradiction between a common hierarchy of occupational prestige in socialist and capitalist societies, on the one hand, and changes in the status of occupations which are associated with the transition from capitalist to state-socialist regimes, on the other. In the former case, the common ordering of a few selected and key occupations gives a positive and high correlation. In the latter case, the abolition of economic classes involves the elimination of old statuses (e.g. landowners) and the creation of new ones (*apparatchiks*) which are ignored for the sake of comparability in the cross-cultural studies. Rather than contradictory sets of facts, the research cited illuminates different aspects of social reality.

A study which attempts to link up the various measures of inequality to form a comprehensive picture of social stratification in state-socialist society has been conducted by Machonin in Czechoslovakia (1970).[7] Machonin identified four main groups in which social position was highly crystallized and three subsidiary groups in which there were inconsistent statuses. These are shown on Figure 1 (p. 85).

Strata A and B are composed of non-manual groups. The first, making up 4·7 per cent of the sample, has a highly consistent profile. Its members have a secondary or university education, are employed in specialized higher professional positions. Such men have highly cultural leisure pursuits, live in towns, have authority in management and command the highest incomes. The second stratum (B) is constituted of lower-grade urban white-collar workers with secondary education, a quite high life-style and income and considerable participation in management.

Strata C and D are manual workers. Stratum C is made up of skilled and semi-skilled industrial workers with elementary education. They have an average cultural level of life-style and low participation in management. Their average income, how-

7. This survey of 13,215 heads of households (0·5 per cent sample) was carried out in 1967.

ever, though below the non-manual groups, is relatively above their scores on other indexes. Stratum D is formed of agricultural workers and semi-skilled and unskilled industrial workers having at most a secondary education, a low income and hardly any participation in management.

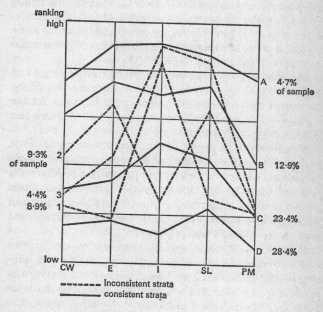

Figure 1. Social strata in Czechoslovakia (1967), based on Machonin (1970, p. 733).

The groups with inconsistent statuses are designated by the figures 1, 2 and 3. Group 1 is made up of semi-skilled or skilled manual workers with elementary education employed in unskilled jobs, with a low style of life rating and a very low index of participation in management. The members of this group, however, have a very high income. Group 2 has a profile which nearly reciprocates that of Group 1. It is composed of lower non-manual workers, particularly clerks in large cities, with lower vocational education and fairly high 'style-of-life' rating. It has a low income and a low index of participation in management. Group 3 follows the pattern of Group 1, being constituted of skilled or semi-skilled workers doing semi-skilled work, with abnormally high incomes and a very high rating of leisure activity, though low participation in management (Machonin, 1970, pp. 735–6).

Machonin's work throws some light on the question which was raised earlier (p. 78) of whether a merging of the white-collar and manual strata has taken place. Despite a relative equalization of incomes, it does not seem to be the case that the distinction between manual and non-manual work has been obliterated. At the top of the social hierarchy (Groups A and B) are two non-manual groups with higher rankings on all dimensions than the bottom two manual groups (C and D). The data from Groups 1 and 2 show that even where industrial workers earn very high incomes and the unskilled white collar very low, their 'style-of-life' index is inverted. Only in Group 3 is there evidence to suggest that manual workers earning very high incomes adopt a style of life or pattern of consumption approximating to that of non-manual strata. This group, however, consists of only 4·6 per cent of the sample and cannot be considered typical. Machonin concludes that 'income equalization . . . was far from leading to corresponding standardization of consumption or of cultural activities during leisure. In brief, the egalitarian arrangement was not such a significant aspects of the social structure as we had assumed . . .' (1970, p. 740).[8] Distinctions of a social kind, particularly life styles, persist between manual and non-manual workers quite independently of levels of skill and of income.

8. Slomczynski, on the basis of 3381 interviews carried out in 1965 and 1967 in Poland has come to a similar conclusion. '*Differences between* [manual and non-manual workers] *at a few variables taken jointly* [education, authority, income and prestige] *are still large*' (1970, p. 25). Italics in original. See Appendix, pp. 138–40.

Sex differentiation

In addition to the ranking of incomes and prestige are two other kinds of inequality: those of sex and ethnic privilege. Sex inequality is often ignored by sociologists because there is a tendency to consider families rather than individuals as units. As Parsons has pointed out, family status is derived from the occupational role of the husband (1954, p. 80). This has been put another way by Engels when he said that the family was founded on 'the open or disguised domestic enslavement of the woman' (1951, p. 211). The role of the woman in Western societies of today has changed significantly compared with that of the woman in the nineteenth-century family which Engels had in mind, mainly because the opportunities outside the traditional roles (wife, mother, daughter) have increased. But in Western capitalist countries even though women enjoy legal equality they are in fact largely excluded from certain occupations. In the mid 1960s, in England for example, women accounted for only 2·9 per cent of solicitors and less than 1 per cent of engineers. Parsons has suggested that role specialization by sex promotes family solidarity and prevents competition between husband and wife. Even when employed outside the home, Parsons asserts that woman's occupations are 'not in direct competition for status with those of men of their own class'. The standards of judgement often applied to women are still related to their personal charm, physical beauty and sexual desirability. Can one say the same about women in state-socialist society?

At first sight, women in the USSR would appear to be more nearly equal to men than is the case in Western capitalist states. Since the early days of the Soviet regime attempts have been made to emancipate women from male domination. Perhaps the best indicators of the changing position of women are their access to higher education and to the occupations traditionally reserved for men. From 1928 to 1935, women's share of the places in institutions of higher education increased from 28 per cent to 38 per cent and by 1941 rose to over 50 per cent (Vol'fson, 1937, p. 186; Fogarty, 1971, pp. 47–98). The proportion has remained just under this figure in the 1960s (Dodge, 1966, pp. 109–11). By 1967 women also accounted for 52 per cent of all professional employees in the USSR, including 72 per cent of the doctors, 68 per cent of the teachers, and 63 per cent of the economists (*Trud v SSSR*, 1968, p. 275). It was during the 1930s that women began to enter a wide range of industrial occupations: in 1928, women constituted 29 per cent of the workers in industry as a whole, whereas by 1969 their proportion had risen to 50 per cent (Smirnov, 1965, p. 351; Tsentral'noe, 1970, p. 536). At the time of the 1897 census, 55 per cent of all employed women were in domestic service, 25 per cent in agriculture, 13 per cent in industry and building and only 4 per cent in the health and educational services. By 1967, 37 per cent of employed women were in industry and building and 25 per cent in health, education and sciences (Zhenshchiny, 1969, p. 83). In the non-European areas of the country, the employment of women increased very markedly under the Soviet regime – eight times in Central Asia and Kazakhstan and nearly five times in Transcaucasia. There can be no doubt then that the impact of Soviet communism has had important effects in changing the social structure by opening up opportunities for women not only in higher education and the professional occupations but also in the middle range of skills previously monopolized by men.

A priori, the higher occupational status of Soviet women in general would imply different relations between the sexes, with greater competition between men and women in those spheres of life which play a major role in determining status. But in fact the standards of judgement are not independent of sex. Even though the cruder exploitation of women in the form of sexually titillating advertising, beauty competitions and strip-tease is strictly banned, milder forms of sex differentiation persist in forms of dress and hair-style and in the use of cosmetics and imply the evaluation of women on criteria outside the occupational status-giving sphere. And in many other ways women's inequality persists. It is still the rule that men take the initiative in the relationships between the sexes: the choosing of partners in Soviet dance halls is usually a male prerogative, overtures for sexual intercourse probably originate from the male (though women's sexual enjoyment has been furthered because the legal and quite widespread practice of abortion has reduced the fear of unwanted children). The family name may legally be adopted from either spouse but in practice it is taken from the male side. But the emancipation of women has not yet led to a significant lightening of her domestic burdens and Soviet studies of the utilization of time have shown that women still bear the brunt of food preparation and domestic cleaning.[9] Women also have less representation among the various elites. Postgraduate women students for instance, made up only 31 per cent of the total of postgraduate students (1946–53), and 25·5 per cent of the total postgraduates in pure science (1962–4). Whereas 25·6 per cent of the total of scientific workers having higher degrees were women, they constituted only 9·4 per cent of the academic elite (Academicians, corresponding members of the Academy and professors) (Tsentral'noe, 1970, p. 694). Though women make up three-fifths of the collective farm workers, in 1956 their share of collective farm chairmanships and state farm directorships came only to 1·9 per cent (Dodge, 1966, pp.136–7, 197, 202). In 1963, only 6 per cent of directors of enterprises, 12 per cent of all heads (and deputies) of workshops and 20 per cent of foreman were women ('Zhenshchiny v S S S R', 1965, p. 93). Women tend to be occupied less in jobs requiring a directional role over men and more in tasks which require specialized knowledge of things.[10] Even in medicine, where men constitute only 15 per cent of all employed in the health service, they occupy 50 per cent of the posts of chief doctors and heads of medical institutions (*Literaturnaya gazeta*, no. 16, 1969, p. 11). In politics, whereas women make up 42·7 per cent of all government deputies, they account for only 28 per cent of the members of the Supreme Soviet (Saifulin, 1967, p. 156). In 1966,

9. A survey in Gorki showed that women spent 40·34 hours per week on housework and shopping etc. whereas the figure for men was 25·45 (Osipov and Frolov, 1966, p. 238).

10. In 1963, 65 per cent of technicians were female, as were 79 per cent of engineer-economists, economists, planners and statisticians.

women accounted for about 20 per cent of Party members and at the Twenty-Third Congress (1966) 23 per cent of the delegates were women; but the figure falls to under 3 per cent when considering the membership of the central committee; and none of the members of the Politbureau is female (*KPSS XXIII* s" *ezd*, 1966).

Thus despite the attempts by the communists to give equality to women, some forms of sexual inequality in the USSR have persisted. It would be superficial to attribute such inequality just to the policy of the communist rulers. The inequality of woman has origins going back to the evolution of man, and beliefs about the inherent differences between sexes and differential expectations of them are passed on unconsciously during the period of childhood socialization. There are also important biological differences between man and woman. Political changes cannot alter the fact that women bear children and laws ignoring biological inequality may not enhance her equality but are likely to increase her possible exploitation by weakening the father's responsibility for the care of his offspring and thereby increasing woman's burdens. These facts have implications of a most subtle kind for authority relations and for responsibility towards children and the home. Furthermore, the very continuation of human society requires harmonious relations between the sexes and the apparently universal role of the male in industrial society as giving status to the family group and as having authority in the family is, as Parsons suggests, probably an adaptive mechanism to reduce rivalry. But there is evidence to suggest that the values of equality of the sexes espoused by socialist ideology have created conflict between married partners in the USSR. Interpretive articles in the Soviet press have commented that one of the main reasons for the increasing amount of divorce in the USSR is the growing aspiration for independence of the individual and the lack of understanding between spouses when woman desires independence and an autonomous career like a man (*Literaturnaya gazeta*, 1 July 1970, p. 11; *Smena*, no. 12, 1970, pp. 6–10). One might anticipate that the implementation of the claims of the contemporary Western

Women's Liberation Movement for greater independence and equality of women may also result in an increase in family breakup unless other fundamental institutional and value changes are also achieved.

Ethnic differences[11]

The Soviet Union is a multi-lingual, multi-racial and multi-national society being composed of many ethnic groups. In the 1970 census, of the 242 million people making up the population of the USSR, 129 millions were Great Russian by nationality; and two other slavic groups, the Ukrainians (forty-one million) and White Russians (nine million) were among the next largest. There were nine other ethnic groups with more than a million people (see Table 12).

It is extremely difficult to determine how far these groups enjoy differential status and prestige or are privileged or under-privileged in respect of political position. The two volumed *Sotsiologiya v SSSR* (1965, 1966) covering Soviet sociological research, has no article on ethnic groups and neither have two recent books on social stratification (*Klassy, sotsial'nye sloi i gruppy v SSSR*, 1968; *Problemy izmeneniya sotsial'noy struktury Sovetskogo obshchestve*, 1968). This reflects the official ideological view:

In our country, live and work in one happy family the representatives of more than a hundred nations and nationalities. In the USSR, for the first time in the history of mankind the nationality problem has been completely resolved (*Strana Sovetov za 50 let: sbornik statisticheskikh materialov*, 1967, p. 19).

Soviet political theory entails the abolition of national *discrimination*, but not of the nation as such. The Soviet writers Rogachev and Sverdlin have defined a nation as:

an historically evolved community of people, characterized by a stable community of economic life (if a working class exists),

11. Ethnic denotes a social group with a diverse range of traits including religious and linguistic characteristics, distinctive skin pigmentation and geographical origin of the members or those of their forebears (Tumin, 1964, pp. 234–4).

Table 12

National Composition of U S S R Population (millions)

	Defined by nationality 1959 Census	1970 Census
Total population	208·82	241·71
Russians	114·11	129·01
Ukrainians	37·25	40·75
White Russians	7·91	9·05
Uzbeks	6·01	9·19
Tatars	4·96	5·93
Kazakhs	3·62	5·29
Azerbaydzhanies	2·93	4·38
Armenians	2·78	3·55
Georgians	2·69	3·24
Lithuanians	2·32	2·66
Jews	2·26	2·15
Moldavians	2·21	2·69
Germans	1·61	1·84
Chuvases	1·46	1·69
Latvians	1·39	1·43
Tadzhiks	1·39	2·13
Poles	1·38	1·16
Mordvinians	1·28	1·26
Turkmenians	1·00	1·52
Bashkirs	0·989	1·24
Estonians	0·988	1·00
Kirgiz	0·968	1·45
Other nationalities*	7	9·10

Sources: Tsentral'noe statisticheskoe upravlenie (1962, pp. 184–9); *Izvestiya*, 17 April 1971.

*Most of the 103 other nationalities are less than a quarter of a million.

territory, language (especially a literary language), and a self-consciousness of ethnic identity, as well as by some specific features of psychology, traditions of everyday life, culture and the struggle for liberation (1966).

Soviet writers distinguish between two kinds of nations: the heterogeneous and the homogeneous. 'Bourgeois nations', it is suggested, are socially *heterogeneous*: they have a bourgeois culture and a 'democratic culture of the working class'. Socialist nations, however, are of a different type; they are *homogeneous*:

The economic basis of socialist nations is public ownership. A most important trait of such nations is their social homogeneity. . . . Here an ethnic community is enhanced by a community of the fundamental socio-political interests of all members of the nation. The ideology of the working class becomes the ideology of the entire nation and the former duality of culture is surmounted. Unlike the socially heterogeneous nations, here arises a genuine and not an artificial community of the destiny of the entire nation (Rogachev and Sverdlin, 1966, pp. 46–7).

Soviet socialist nations are considered to be of this kind. From this viewpoint, they are based on brotherhood, the distinctions between them are held to be cultural in character and thus membership of a 'socialist nation' does *not* bestow inequality, social superiority or inferiority, but simply distinctions of a cultural and linguistic kind; in short, nationality involves differentiation rather than stratification.

Another important aspect of this attitude to nation is the implication that international conflict ceases to exist between socialist nations. The argument runs that 'bourgeois nations' pursue the policies of their ruling classes, whereas 'socialist nations' having no ruling class are able to follow peaceful policies. Many Western commentators deny the validity of this theory and argue that international conflict between socialist nations is not withering away. It may be caused by disagreements between such nations over economic exchange, over cultural dominance or over territory though these problems lie outside the scope of the present text. The extent of ethnic inequality in state-socialist societies, however, is of concern.

It would be surprising if there were equality of treatment of ethnic groups in the USSR. The Bolsheviks inherited a system of severe inequality between nationalities. Before the Revolution in Central Asia, for example, only some 2 to 3 per cent of the native population was literate (Wheeler, 1964,

p. 97), there were no institutions of higher learning and industrial development had hardly begun. The Soviet government attempted to reduce industrial and cultural inequalities and large-scale industry was set up in the underdeveloped areas. Between 1913 and 1935 in Turkmenia the industrial output of large-scale industry increased eight-fold, in Kazakhstan 8·5 times and in Kirgizin 83 times whereas the figure for the USSR as a whole was 5·7 times (Schlesinger, 1956, p. 260). Despite the inadequacies of the statistics and the low base, there has been a remarkable growth of industry in these previously backward areas though there are still considerable inequalities between the national groups. In 1961 while per capita income was 100 in Latvia, it was 47·7 in Uzbekistan and 41·8 in Tadzhikistan (Nove and Newth, 1967, p. 42).

Educational provision has followed a similar trend. The non-Russian peoples have increased their chances of education, but have not yet reached the level of the Russians. In 1959, for instance, 28·1 per cent of the total Soviet population had received a minimum of seven years education: of Kazakhs the figure was 18·2 per cent; of Uzbeks 20·8 per cent; of Kirgiz 19·9 per cent; Tadzhiks 20·1 per cent and Turkmens, 24·2 per cent (Nove, p. 72). Aspaturian has calculated an index of the national composition of students in higher education (see Table 13). A figure over 1 denotes over-representation, and an index below 1 shows under-representation. The Tadzhiks, Kirgiz, Turkmens and Uzbeks have obviously bettered their national chances for higher education. Some groups are still relatively more privileged – Russians, Kazakhs, Georgians, Armenians and Jews. It ought to be noted that (even though their index fell) the total number of Jewish students rose from 51,600 in 1956 to 94,600 in 1965. The Soviet authorities have enhanced the chances of the non-Russian nationalities for higher education by instituting a nationality quota system which tries to ensure a fairer balance between the national groups than would be the case if qualifications alone were considered. While this practice has been the subject of criticism in the West it is probably necessary if recruitment of underprivileged groups is to be improved.

Table 13

Index of Student Composition by Nationality 1927, 1959, 1965

Nationality	Index 1927	Index 1959	Index 1965
Russian	1·06	1·13	1·11
Ukrainian	0·69	0·75	0·81
Uzbek	0·11	0·82	0·83
Kazakh	0·07	0·94	1·06
Georgian	2·00	1·41	1·38
Azerbaydzhani	0·91	0·92	0·93
Kirgiz	0·12	1·00	0·80
Tadzhik	0·08	0·71	0·57
Armenian	1·81	1·07	1·14
Turkmen	0·21	0·80	0·80
Jewish	7·50	3·73	2·18
Tatar	0·40	0·75	0·71

Source: Aspaturian (1968, p. 177).

The figures mentioned ignore the quality of education institution attended. Because the more prestigious institutes and universities are located in the European parts of the Russian Republic it is probable that they contain a lower than average proportion of the non-Russian nationalities. In addition to this, other kinds of traditional barriers to educational equality still linger so that, for example, while in 1960 the percentage of female students for the USSR was 43 per cent, among the Muslim nationalities it was only 26 per cent (Nove and Newth, 1967, p. 73).

Let us now turn to consider the relations between the most numerous Russian ethnic group and the others. Patterns of interaction between slavic and non-slavic groups have not been the subject of much study in the USSR. However, a study by Arutyunyan based on 2500 interviews conducted in the Tatar Autonomous Republic, sheds some useful light on the attitudes of Russians and Tatars to authority positions and to intermarriage. When asked: 'If you were given an opportunity to select a person in direct command over you, which [nationality] would you prefer?' Of those speaking only the Tatar language 12 per cent preferred a man of Tatar nationality whereas only 3·6 per cent of those speaking Russian preferred a person of their own nationality. When asked, 'Do you approve of marriages between Tatars and Russians? How would you regard such a marriage by one of your near kin (son, daughter, brother or sister)?' Of the Tatars, only 0·4 per cent considered such a match objectionable, compared to 3·6 per cent of the Russians. A further 14·9 per cent of the Tatars and 5·4 per cent of the Russians preferred marriage to take place between persons of similar nationalities but would not raise any objection to a mixed marriage. At the other end of the scale 80·4 per cent of Russians and 69·4 per cent of Tatars believed that the nationality of spouses had no significance. Some interesting differences are brought out when the ethnic groups are sub-divided into men and women, and into intelligentsia and other workers. Of the Tatar male intelligentsia, 13·6 per cent had a negative attitude both to a direct boss being of a different national-ethnic group and to mixed marriages, whereas among the Russian male intelligentsia, the proportions were 5·8 per cent and 14·7 per cent respectively. An even higher percentage of Tatar women who were also intelligentsia were opposed to these arrangements: 18·5 per cent had a negative attitude to being supervised by a Russian and 14·2 per cent were opposed to mixed marriages. Russian women of intellectual status also felt just as strongly about mixed marriage as did their Tatar counterparts, 14·2 per cent having a negative attitude, but only 9·8 per cent of them were opposed to having a direct supervisor of Tatar nationality. By contrast with the male intelligentsia, male workers were less prejudiced: of the Tatars, 9·3 per cent had a negative attitude to a person of a different nationality being in command over them, and 11·0 per cent felt similarly about mixed marriages; and among the Russian male workers the proportion fell to 2·8 per cent on both counts. Tatar women workers, on the other hand, had the highest 'negative scores' of all groups: 17·7 per cent had a negative attitude to having a Russian supervisor and 15·6 were against mixed marriages; of the Russian women workers the figures were much lower – 3·8 per cent and 7·6 per cent respectively (Arutyunyan, 1969, pp. 133–4).

The figures cited above sustain the view that there is mild social prejudice between national/racial groups in the USSR, and that it is greater among the Tatars than the Russians. One may confidently conclude that a fair number of Tatars do not like being told what to do by Russians, and that a minority regard intermarriage with some distaste. The research also indicates that social class cuts across ethnic origin and is a most significant variable in understanding inter-ethnic group relations.

Let us now turn to consider the political aspects of the nationality problem. To what extent, it might be asked, do the slavic white nations dominate the others? Brzezinski and Huntington have suggested that the counterpart of the United States' WASPS (White Anglo-Saxon Protestants) are the SRAPPS (Slavic-stock Russian-born Apparatchiks) (1964, pp. 132–3). Their grounds are that this ethnic group has superior access to positions of economic and political power and takes the most important decisions affecting the life of society. How valid is such a statement? Bialer has shown that Russians clearly dominate in the elite positions (1966). The ethnic composition of the Politbureau-Presidium and Secretariat of the CPSU between 1919 and 1935 and between 1939 and 1963 is shown in Table 14 (p. 98).

The predominance of Russians, the rise of Ukrainians and the massive relative decline of the Jews are the main facts brought out by the table: of the central apparatus of the party in September 1963, the Russians and Ukrainians made up seventy-one out of the total membership of seventy-two (p. 211). In 1966, the Slavic nationalities constituted 81·5 per cent of the CPSU central committee, and 83·3 per cent of the Politbureau and Secretariat: their share of the population as a whole was 76·3 per cent (Bilinsky, 1967, pp. 23–5). Of seventy-nine government officials in the Council of Ministers in May 1964, sixty were Russians, sixteen Ukrainians and three had other ethnic origins and of forty-seven ministers in the Council in 1966, thirty-nine were Russians, six Ukrainians, one was a

Table 14

Ethnic Composition of Politbureau-Presidium and
CPSU Secretariat

Nationality	1919–35 (N = 34)	1939–63 (N = 58)
	as percentage	as percentage
Russian	65	79
Ukrainian	0	10
Georgian	6	3
Armenian	3	2
Uzbek	0	2
Jewish	18	2
Finn	0	2
Latvian	0	0
Polish	3	0

Source: Bialer (1966, p. 217).

Tatar and there was one Armenian (*Deputaty verkhovnogo
soveta SSSR*, 1966). Of fifty-six senior managers of the Soviet
economy who were elected to the Central Committee at the
Twenty-Second Congress (1961), forty-five (80 per cent) were
Russians, nine (16 per cent) were Ukrainians, one (4 per cent)
was a White Russian and another was a Jew (Bialer, 1966).

At lower levels of the power system, the representation of
non-Russian nationalities is much higher. Bilinsky has shown
that in 1966 the First Secretary of each of the Republican
Communist Parties was a national of the indigenous population. Similarly, members of the Republican Politbureaux were
largely men of the indigenous nationality: for example in
Uzbekistan, seven out of ten were Uzbeks and in Latvia, seven
out of ten were Latvians (Bilinsky, 1967, p. 20). All the Chairmen of Councils of Ministers in the Union Republics were
members of the titular nationality and so were the First
Deputy Chairmen in thirteen out of fifteen cases (Bialer, 1966).

On the basis of such a short review, one cannot come to very
firm conclusions about ethnic stratification in the USSR.
While the occupation of political elite positions is biased in
favour of the dominant Russian nationality, at local levels this

balance is redressed. On the other hand, there is some evidence to suggest that ethnic groups may be at a disadvantage in the economic and educational spheres but the view that certain ethnic groups are subject to a form of severe social under-privilege cannot be sustained.[12] In social relations, it is again probably true that there is a mild form of social discrimination on national ethnic lines.

Subjective evaluation of status

So far the statistics we have considered are only indirectly relevant to social interaction. When asked, people may say that certain occupations confer social esteem but we must also consider the way in which these attitudes are reflected in social relations and social action. To what extent do manual workers defer to professional men? In what ways, if any, are women treated in an inferior manner to men? It might be the case, for instance, that even though ranking of individuals by pro-fession is similar in two societies, the actual social distance between the compared occupations is very different. Members of an officer corps or the civil service may be given an equally high 'ranking' but the consciousness of having the status of an officer or of a permanent civil servant might well vary. The specific authority of occupational roles may have very dif-ferent consequences for other role positions. Obviously, the extent to which roles reinforce each other is an important element in social stratification. The fact that a person has an upper professional occupation or is high on a certain ranking scale (income) does not necessarily mean that he will be de-ferred to or be given respect by all those who have lower positions or incomes. Here then we are concerned with the impact of the division of labour on other social relations.

This is a crucial aspect of social stratification into which very little systematic research has been carried out. It requires

12. Anti-Russian sentiments are, of course, forbidden, as are move-ments in favour of local national independence. During the war seven nationalities were deported on the grounds of security to Siberia and Central Asia. This policy was officially denounced in the late 1950s (Conquest, 1967, pp. 102–8).

not the description of objective inequalities but consideration of how people rank others and themselves, and examination of how in practice incumbents of given roles relate to one another, of an analysis of how superiority and inferiority are reflected in social activity. The value system of a society defines in broad terms the desirable modes of action: Christians should play the good Samaritan to the downtrodden, Soviet communists should have relations of 'mutual respect between individuals – man is to man a friend, comrade and brother' (Programme of the Communist Party of the Soviet Union, 1961, p. 79). In the Soviet value system, it is axiomatic that particular occupations or levels of income should not elevate some men over others. In *theory*, individuals are merely differentiated from one another and not stratified in terms of social worth. In other words, the status and role of an individual in relation to the means of production and exchange should not, in a socialist form of society, give rise to a consciousness of membership of a social stratum (or class) which shares common values, attitudes and interests, and which considers itself as superior or inferior to other strata. Ideological statements, however, are no sure indication of the way individuals or groups do act. Soviet sociologists have been concerned with the development of a socialist personality, with a 'new socialist man' (*Dukhovoe razvitie lichnosti*, 1967). Their writings have concentrated on the educational and cultural levels of different social groups, rather than on the interaction between individuals and groups and their differential perception of the social structure. Though it would be interesting to describe the statuses of individuals in different positions, no Soviet work has been carried out into these relationships. It is possible, however, to gain some insight into these aspects of Soviet life from contemporary Soviet literature and expatriates; and from such accounts there would appear to be considerable conflict between the professions and political groups, between youth and the older generation, between those in authority and those subject to authority.

One may also make some inferences about the nature of social relations by studying patterns of friendship and marriage. It might be expected that in an egalitarian society friendship and marriage would be formed independently of occupation, educational background or level of income. On the other hand, if friendship networks and intermarriage occurred predominantly between those of similar social background, this would indicate the existence of social barriers and social distance between groups.

The occupational groups of spouses according to a social survey conducted in Hungary in 1963 are shown on Table 15 (p. 102) (Hungarian Central Statistical Office, 1967). As the data refer to the actual occupations of spouses after marriage, they are of limited use concerning social mobility. However, we may infer from the table that the overwhelming majority of spouses share the same occupational social status: 65 per cent of the non-manual husbands took non-manual wives and 70 per cent of the non-manual women took non-manual husbands; 50 per cent of the industrial-manual men had industrial-manual wives, and 80 per cent of women with industrial-manual jobs had husbands of the same occupation; of agricultural-manual men, 96 per cent had taken wives in the same occupational category, and 59 per cent of agricultural-manual women workers had agricultural-manual spouses.

A Soviet study of educational attainment of spouses showed a high positive correlation ($+0.66$). It was found that 93·4 per cent of the men with higher education had married women with middle and higher education and at the other end of the scale, 65·2 per cent of men with less than elementary education had married women at the same educational level (Aganbegyan, 1966, pp. 200–201).[13] Again a Polish study of the educational backgrounds of 1401 married couples found that spouses had very similar educational backgrounds. Of women with higher education, 87 per cent had husbands of the same educational standing, and 93 per cent of the wives of men with incomplete primary education had received a complete primary (25 per

13. In a study of 1000 Leningrad divorces, 77·3 per cent of the couples belonged to the same social group which, if it is at all representative of all marriages, confirms the above, Kharchev (1965, p. 163).

Table 15

Intermarriage by Occupational Groups, Hungary 1963

	Wives Non-manual	*Industrial-manual*	*Agricultural-manual*	*Totals*
Husbands Non-manual	65 *800* 70	24 *295* 16	11 *131* 4	100 *1226*
Industrial-manual	12 *344* 30	50 *1433* 80	38 *1109* 37	100 *2886*
Agricultural-manual	0 *0* 0	4 *66* 4	96 *1759* 59	100 *1825*
Totals	*1144* 100	*1794* 100	*2999* 100	*5937*

Source: Hungarian Central Statistical Office (1967, p. 126).

cent) or incomplete primary (68 per cent) education (Lobodzinska, 1970, p. 8).

A Hungarian study of graduate engineers shows that they mainly make friends with people of a similar educational and professional background: as many as 86 per cent of young chemical engineers' best friends were graduates mostly engaged in similar professions. The same study confirms that marriage takes place between spouses of similar occupational backgrounds. The wives of the chemical engineers were also largely selected from similar occupational groups (Szesztay, 1967, pp. 154–5).

We may conclude that in state socialist societies no less than in Western ones there is significant differentiation of interest and outlook between people from various backgrounds which strongly influences their choices of friends and spouses. The high rates of marriage within certain occupational groups together with the evidence from the research (see pp. 108–16) on the aspirations of children would also suggest that the off-spring of different strata are socialized into quite different sub-cultures.

Let us now turn to consider how individuals perceive class position. Research into the perception of class position was conducted in Poland in 1958 and was based on a sample of workers in six industrial enterprises and five other groups (the Ministry of Education, a hospital clinic, and craftsmen, sailors and young people at a youth camp). Of those objectively 'working class', 92·6 per cent considered themselves to be of that class. The ideology bestowing prestige on workers prob-ably accounts for this very high figure. Of the 'intelligentsia' who had come from this background, 79 per cent considered themselves to be 'intelligentsia'; on the other hand, of the intelligentsia who originated in the manual strata, only 37·6 per cent considered themselves to be members of the intel-ligentsia, the majority assigning themselves to the 'working class' (Widerszpil, 1959). What makes the Polish results even more remarkable is the fact that the surveys were carried out only fourteen years after the creation of a state-socialist society. Of course, in the Polish countryside the peasantry would prob-ably not have identified themselves as 'working class' to the same extent as non-manual workers.

The Polish sociologists also investigated people's percep-tions of the number and character of social classes. The largest group of respondents (34·5 per cent) identified three classes: workers, peasants, intelligentsia. The next largest grouping (16·3 per cent) defined 'two classes without significant con-tradictions' (classes not specified). The existence of a 'ruling class' was mentioned in only 14·6 per cent of the responses. Thus the 'official' perception of social reality seems to have been internalized to a considerable extent in the people's consciousness although there were differences in social imagery depending on the occupational status of the respondents. 34·7 per cent of the workers, 41·5 per cent of the clerks in industry, 23·6 per cent of the technical intelligentsia and 70·2 per cent of vocational school graduates thought that there were three groups – workers, peasantry and the intelligentsia. A significant number (47·1 per cent) of clerical assistants employed in government offices perceived a four-class scheme: workers, peasants, intelligentsia and a group in private business. 'Private business' (i.e. people such as retailers and craftsmen working on their own account) was mentioned in just over a quarter of the replies of the total sample. The notion of a 'ruling class' was spread evenly through the responses: it was mentioned in one combination or another by 15 per cent of the workers, 11 per cent of industrial clerks, 18 per cent of technical intelligentsia. There was no significant difference between party members and non-party respondents in this respect, 12 per cent of the former and 13 per cent of the latter having a conception of this category.

A further aspect of social differentiation, on which again there are no Soviet data, is the attitude of different social groups towards wage inequality. However, the results of a Polish survey which bears on this problem may be summarized as follows (Glowacki, 1959). The 'great majority' of manual workers thought that the government should set limits to wage differentials and believed that the existing differentiation in Poland was both too great and was unjustified. Examples of the kinds of argument favoured by these relatively lowly paid egalitarians are that 'everyone has the same stomach and same right to live', and that 'a director and a cleaner have the same needs'. Some of them also advanced explicitly political arguments of the following kind: 'as all are to be equal under communism so wages should not differ'; 'a too high differentiation in wages divides into classes which as time passes are becoming hostile to each other'; 'the worker under communism should not be so badly treated'. The majority of technical and administrative personnel was also in favour of limiting wage differentials, but here a sizeable minority (one fifth) was against such a policy. The views of the majority also exhibited more varied and sophisticated reasons: such as that 'the difficulties arising for the state should be equally spread over all citizens', and that 'everyone tries to fulfil his duties well, so wages should not differ much'. But the majority of the technical administrative group wanted greater differentials between lowest and highest incomes than did the manual workers; and those who opposed an upper limit argued that the existing limits were insufficient incentive for maximum effort. The third group of respondents, those with higher education, tended to favour both higher differentials (from 5:1 to 10:1) and even the removal of a ceiling. The arguments they used are familiar in Western societies: 'it is necessary to have incentives for greater effort and [to enhance] educational improvement'; 'it is worth giving a few thousand more to a good director or engineer [for] the profits may be in millions'; 'in building and industry the difference is too little and even in an opposite direction from what it should be'. As Glowacki points out, personal conditions had an indubitable relationship to egalitarianism: the lower the income and education, the greater the claims for egalitarianism; and the higher the education and income, the greater the wish for hierarchy.

Estimations of social worth also varied by social class. Manual workers believed that miners and foundry workers deserved the highest salaries – higher even than those of scientists, other experts and political leaders. The technical and administrative personnel (without higher education) put in first place highly qualified experts, then scientists, factory managers, political leaders. The engineers and other personnel with higher education would have given the highest salaries to scientists, the creative intelligentsia and those in leading government posts – in that order; and very few of this group ranked miners and foundry workers at all highly.

This research from Poland thus highlights the conflicts that exist over the distribution of the economic surplus between the various social strata. After the initial political process by which the capitalist owners of industry were expropriated, conflicts arise between the new elites (including the highly qualified professional groups and the party apparat) and the majority of the manual workers. The latter invoke 'communist ideology' to support egalitarian wage claims which would give them benefits, while the intelligentsia seek to further their cause by reference to their superior contribution to the national welfare. Even those in intermediate positions rationalize their own self interest by reference to general social goals. These empirical facts point up a contradiction between the 'official ideology', according to which the 'working class' is politically and socially unitary, and the fact that income is distributed differentially between various groups making up that class. At the same time it is interesting to note that these groups are able to articulate more or less opposing views which rationalize their different interests, despite the unifying objective of the official ideology.

On the basis of the evidence presented above we may make a number of observations which modify the 'official' Soviet view of social stratification. Although income inequality in state-socialist countries of the Soviet type has a narrower span than in capitalist societies, there is, nevertheless, a considerable variation in the actual consumption patterns of different social strata which indicates a marked differentiation of life styles. Status differentiation appears to be related very closely to occupation and education and while the range of 'social distance' may be narrower in state-socialist countries than in Western capitalist states (though this has not been very satisfactorily proven) a generally similar rank ordering of occupations occurs. Inequalities between the sexes and between nationalities also persist. Furthermore, what facts we have about patterns of marriage and perceptions of differential rewards strongly suggest that state-socialist societies do have a definite system of prestige and that individuals regard themselves as members of distinctive status groups.

5 Social Mobility and Political Class

The foregoing chapter has been concerned with the hierarchical arrangement of social groups and with the nature of inequalities between them. We shall now turn to consider the extent to which such differences may have crystallized to form more enduring social groups. The theoretical implications of this problem have been outlined in chapter 2 and in the present chapter we shall use what empirical material there is available to test whether a ruling class or political elite is ensconced at the apex of the power structure. It might be objected, of course, that it is not possible to 'test' such general theories in a short text for they require a profound analysis over time of many aspects of the society we are describing and, in addition, much crucial information is not available in systematic and reliable form. However, despite these objections, we might consider two indicators of group crystallization. Firstly, we may study the extent to which upper professional and executive occupations are open to recruitment from manual and unskilled non-manual strata. Secondly, we may examine the social composition of the political elites which will give us some indication of the extent to which there exist self-perpetuating ruling groups.

The recruitment of the intelligentsia

A characteristic of a democratic occupational structure is that leading and intellectual occupations are both desired and actually open to all children independently of their social background. One might expect, other things being equal, that the distribution of children in professional occupations would *not* vary with the occupation of their fathers. Social mobility should provide avenues for upward and downward movement such that one social group would not monopolize the desirable positions.

One of the most comprehensive studies of the relationship between parents' occupation and children's occupational choice has been conducted in Hungary in 1963 (Hungarian Central Statistical Office, 1967). Some of the crucial figures are summarized on Table 16. This shows in the first column, the occupations of heads of households and two other sets of data: the actual careers in non-manual jobs of their children and the aspirations of parents for the children still studying for non-manual work.

Four inferences may be made from the table. First, we see that of the *employed* children, those with parents in higher professional positions had very high chances of obtaining higher professional and non-manual occupations: 69 per cent of the higher professional households had children with careers in non-manual occupations. At the other end of the scale, only 4 per cent of the households of the bottom category (agricultural workers) had children in non-manual occupations. Secondly, parents' *aspirations* for their children were closely correlated to the occupation of head of household. While of skilled workers' households 29 per cent wanted professional jobs for all their children, the comparable figure rose to 68 per cent of the higher professionals. Thirdly, despite the social differences, the general trend emerges that, among all social strata, there were higher expectations for children than actual past achievement would seem to warrant. Fourthly, while the lower occupational groups did proportionately worse than the higher, there was still considerable movement from manual occupations into non-manual.

A Polish survey[1] has attempted to compare social mobility in pre-war and post-war Poland. A summary of some of the results is shown in Table 17. The table shows that, comparing the situation before the war with that between 1956 and 1968, a large increase took place in both the proportions of in-

1. A sample consisting of 3482 non-agricultural households conducted in 1968 (Zagorski, 1970).

Table 16

Parents' Aspirations for their Children and their Actual Careers, Hungary 1963

	Actual careers				Aspired to careers			
Occupation of head of household (pensioners excluded)	Percentage of households in which:				Percentage of households in which parents of children still studying desire:			
	all children are in higher professional occupations	all children are in higher professional and other non-manual occupations	all have non-manual but not higher professional occupations	Total non-manual	for all their children higher professional occupations	for all their children higher professional and other non-manual occupations	for all their children non-manual but not higher professional occupations	Total non-manual
Persons in higher professional occupations	22	7	40	69	68	6	15	89
Other non-manual occupations	9	4	40	53	55	6	18	79
Skilled workers	3	2	25	30	29	5	23	57
Unskilled workers	2	1	10	13	14	2	17	33
Agricultural cooperative members	1	1	6	8	20	3	16	39
Agricultural workers	1	0	3	4	13	2	11	26

Source: Based on Ferge (1966).

dustrial manual and non-manual workers hailing from a farming background: for the former the proportion rose from 22 per cent before 1940 to 39·9 per cent between 1956 and 1968; the share of children from agricultural backgrounds taking non-manual work rose from 18·3 per cent to 30·5 per cent. The share of non-manual workers with fathers in industrial-manual work only rose slightly from 24·2 per cent before the war to 26·1 per cent between 1956 and 1958. Movement from non-manual into manual jobs, however, was very small, rising only from 4 per cent to 5·7 per cent between the pre- and post-war periods, showing that the children of non-manual parents tend to stay in non-manual jobs. Upward social mobility, therefore, has been stimulated by the increase in non-manual and manual jobs outside agriculture resulting in a general upward movement of men from industrial manual and agricultural backgrounds, rather than a large downward movement of non-manual strata.

Turning to educational opportunity, we find that in Poland, children of non-manual social background still form the largest group of students. In 1960–61 they accounted for 46·5 per cent of the total number of students in higher education (Sarapata, 1966, p. 46). By 1967–8, the share of first year students originating from such strata rose to 54·3 per cent of the total though the proportion fell back to 48·4 per cent in 1969–70 (Zagorski, 1970, p. 11). In Poland then, as in Hungary, there is a much greater probability of non-manual workers' children entering non-manual work and higher education than there is for the offspring of manual workers; though, at the same time, quite a large share of non-manual workers originate from manual family background.

Soviet research, while not as comprehensive as the Polish or as detailed as the Hungarian, paints a similar picture. A survey conducted by Shubkin (1965, 1966) shows not only that it is the intelligentsia who have the highest aspirations for their offspring but that the actual achievement of their children outstrips that of other social groups. Another study conducted in Sverdlovsk shows that 89 per cent of parents employed as 'specialists' wanted higher education for their children, whereas

Table 17

First Jobs as Manual or Non-manual Workers outside Agriculture according to Fathers' Socio-Occupational Group at that Time (Poland)

Father's socio-occupational group	Respondent's socio-occupational group when taking first job			
	Industrial-manual workers		Non-manual workers	
	Year work was commenced			
	Before 1940	1956–69	Before 1940	1956–68
	%	%	%	%
Farmers or agricultural labourers	22·0	39·9	18·3	30·5
Manual workers outside agriculture	66·3	48·1	24·2	26·1
Non-manual workers	4·0	5·7	43·3	36·4
Private handicraftsmen etc.	4·3	2·1	9·2	2·6
No data	3·4	4·2	5·0	4·4
	100·0	100·0	100·0	100·0
N	323	700	120	341

Source: Adapted from Zagorski (1970, p. 4).

the figures for workers and collective farmers were 64·9 per cent and 36·2 per cent respectively (Tkach, 1967, p. 145). Also, non-manual children secured a disproportional share of the places in higher education. Further evidence is provided by Rutkevich who cites the following statistics on the social background of students at institutions of higher education in Sverdlovsk. Study of Table 18 shows that in 1964 the majority of full-time, and in 1959 the greater share of evening-course, students in Sverdlovsk were recruited from manual-worker social origins; but at other times and by all kinds of study, students of non-manual origin were relatively and absolutely

Table 18

Social Background of Students in Higher Education
in Sverdlovsk by Form of Study

Social origin	Population of Sverdlovsk Province	Form of study					
		Day (full-time)		Evening		Correspond- ence	
	1959	1959	1964	1959	1964	1959	1964
Manual workers	70	46·7	52·4	57·2	46·4	37·2	38·4
Peasants	8	5·5	7·2	0·1*	2·9*	11·0	8·2
Non-manual workers	22	47·8	40·4	42·7	51·7	51·8	53·4
	100	100·0	100·0	100·0	101·0	100·0	100·0

* No evening study was available at the agricultural institute in Sverdlovsk.

Source: *Klassy, sotsial'nye sloi i gruppy v SSSR* (1968, p. 209).

in the ascendancy, despite the fact that the share of non-manual workers in the population as a whole was as low as 22 per cent.[2]

A more detailed study showing the social background of students by educational institutions reveals some interesting facts (see Table 19). Study of this table not only confirms what was said above on unequal class chances, but it also shows the prevalence of certain social groups in particular faculties. Students from white-collar homes are particularly well represented at the university, the law institute, teachers' institute and conservatory. Those from working-class background are more frequent at the polytechnic, the mining, the railway and the economics institute. Though these figures refer to correspondence and evening-course students, among all students a similar tendency operates. Figures for Sverdlovsk province

2. In Byelorussia, it has been found that the share of students at the technological institute with non-manual backgrounds rose from 29·1 per cent in 1963 to 46 per cent in 1967 and at the agricultural institute their share rose from 21·7 per cent to 25·7 per cent. At the medical institute the share of non-manuals fell from 53 per cent in 1964 to 51·4 per cent in 1969 (*Struktura Sovetskoy intelligentsii*, 1970, pp. 66, 89).

Table 19

Social Background of Students in Higher Education by, Institution and form of Study, Sverdlovsk 1966

Institution	Evening Students				Correspondence Students			
	N	Manual workers or children of manual workers %	Peasants or children of peasants %	Non-manual workers or children of non-manual %	N	Manual workers or children of manual workers %	Peasants or children of peasants %	Non-manual workers or children of non-manual %
Polytechnic	5913	63·8		36·2	9073	45·2		54·8
Mining institute	929	54·9	2·6	42·5	4018	58·4	0·4	41·2
University	2069	21·7	0·6	77·7	2692	34·8	10·2	55·0
Railway institute	1534	64·1		35·9	4277	38·3		61·7
Law institute	1027	37·4		62·9	4868	17·2		82·5
Economics institute	170	57·1	5·3	37·6	1810	51·1	0·3	48·8
Teachers' institute	277	31·8		68·2	3015	3·5	0·1	96·5
Conservatory	82	24·4	3·7	71·9	248	35·9		64·1
Totals	12001	52·5	0·4	47·1	30001	36·6	0·9	63·5

Source: *Protsessy izmeneniya sotsial'noy struktury v Sovetskom obschestve* (1967, pp. 133, 139).

show that 70 to 73 per cent of students at industrial and building institutes originated from the manual-working class, whereas in cultural institutes (music, art, etc.) the proportion was 50 to 52 per cent (*Protsessy izmeneniya sotsial'noy struktury v Sovetskom obshchestve*, 1967, p. 125). Therefore, it might be inferred that relatively more upward mobility takes place for manual workers in industrial than in non-industrial occupations. This is illustrated by a study of occupational mobility in a Moscow electrical engineering plant which showed that of a thousand workers who began as semi-skilled operators, after ten years, 295 were engineers or technicians and 680 skilled operators. Of thirty-four men who had entered the factory ten years previously as apprentices, fourteen had been promoted to the position of engineer or technician (Guryanov, 1966, p. 127).

Another study of first year students at the Urals University in 1963 found that in the physics faculty 58 per cent of the students came from 'specialists' families, in biology the figure was 41·6 per cent and in mathematics 31 per cent. In the less prestigious subjects (economics, journalism and history) it was much lower, ranging from 11·6 per cent to 21·5 per cent (*Klassy, sotsial'nye sloi i gruppy*, 1968, p. 211). It seems probable then that employment opportunities, coupled with part-time study, encourage the social mobility of young workers through the study of 'applied' subjects – railway engineering, mining, etc. In pure science subjects, such as maths and physics, the cultural background would seem to give an advantage to the children of parents who have a higher education and who are engaged in creative or administrative work.[3] Outside industry, upward social mobility is probably greatest in the lower professions (economics, journalism, school teaching) which recruit many children from manual working-class background.

3. Also, in the higher creative arts the children of non-manual workers do well. Of members of artistic professional associations in Byelorussia 77 per cent of composers, 68·9 per cent of architects, 59 per cent of cinema professionals, 47 per cent of painters and 25 per cent of writers has non-manual origins (*Struktura Sovetskoy intelligentsii*, 1970, p. 104).

Within the upper professional occupations, there is considerable horizontal mobility and mainly in the direction of scientific and technological employment in the sons' generation. Seventy-three per cent of sons where fathers had graduated in the humanities aspired to posts in physics, mathematics and technology, 22 per cent to other natural sciences and only 5 per cent to jobs in social science, history, literature and language. Of sons having fathers with professional qualifications in physics, maths and technology, 88 per cent aspired to their father's professions, 12 per cent to other natural sciences and none wanted a career in the humanities. Girls of higher professional origin, on the other hand, were more attracted to the humanities. Of the daughters of mathematicians, physicists and technologists, 39 per cent wanted the same profession, 29 per cent other scientific jobs, and 30 per cent preferred the humanities; whereas among daughters with fathers in the humanities, 50 per cent wanted a similar profession, while 21 per cent preferred physics, maths, technology and 26 per cent other scientific professions (Aganbegyan, 1966, p. 221). This is probably explained by the fact that the status of a family is determined by the position of the husband; men, therefore, aspire to the prestigious scientific jobs, whereas girls give these less priority.

Let us now turn to consider the ways that the school and the family influence children's success in the educational system. Since Soviet schools are unstreamed and comprehensive, the structure of the school would appear to be egalitarian. In theory, the school seeks to raise all children up to a common average standard. Children from poorer home backgrounds, therefore, might be thought to benefit most from this system while those from a superior intellectual home environment may not be fully extended. But despite the comprehensive-school system there is considerable difference in the attainment of children and Aganbegyan, Osipov and Shubkin (1966) have shown that success at school is correlated with parents' education and social position. For boys, the correlation coefficient relating success at school and mothers' occupation is $+0.31$, and for girls the correlation between mothers' education and school success is +0·32 (p. 204). A study in Novosibirsk which related children's school grades to their social background showed that the offspring of parents with higher educational qualifications did much better than those of other social groups: on average 5 per cent of all children got 'excellent' marks but this figure rose to 11·4 per cent in the case of the children of parents with higher education, and the comparative figures for 'good' marks were 30·5 per cent and 43 per cent for the two groups respectively (Musatov, 1967, p. 47).

As in Western societies, home background also influences the age at which children leave school. In Nizhny Tagil it was found that children of workers made up 72 per cent of the school intake, 60 per cent of the eighth form, 55 per cent of the ninth form and 44·2 per cent of the eleventh form (*Klassy, sotsial'nye sloi i gruppy*, 1968, pp. 206–7). The Hungarian survey (Ferge, 1966) mentioned above strikingly brings out the unequal statum chances of staying in education: while 83 per cent of children of the upper professional group remained at school after the compulsory minimum age, this figure fell to 37 per cent for the children of skilled workers, to 15 per cent for those of unskilled workers, and to 18 per cent for those of agricultural labourers.

The above discussion has centred on the accessibility of rather general statuses, such as non-manual work, and particular occupations. But even higher professional occupations are stratified, having eminent groups, or elites, which have honour and authority in a limited sphere. One of the most comprehensive studies of national elites has been conducted in Yugoslavia between 1967 and 1969. The researchers studied 517 leading 'opinion-makers' drawn from legislators, 'prominent parliamentary deputies', federal administrators, political leaders (party central committee and other socio-political groups), economic leaders (economic planners and leading factory directors), mass communicators (editors and directors of radio and TV, prominent broadcasters and journalists) and intellectuals (professors in social sciences, prominent authors, literary critics, film directors). A summary of the results is shown in Table 20.

Table 20

Fathers' Occupations of Public Opinion Makers (Yugoslavia 1968) (by sectors)

Fathers' occupations	Sector Legislators	Administrators	Political leaders	Economic leaders	Journalists	Intellectuals	Total	Yugoslav population as a whole 1961
Non-manual occupations	26·1	40·0	26·3	22·4	50·4	58·6	39·2	18·9
Manual workers	35·4	33·3	40·8	44·4	24·8	29·8	34·0	31·9
Agricultural workers	33·8	24·4	27·6	27·2	16·8	9·6	22·1	49·2
Others	4·6	2·2	5·2	6·0	8·0	2·0	4·7	
	100·0	100·0	100·0	100·0	100·0	100·0	100·0	100·0
N	65	90	76	81	104	101	517	

Source: Based on *International Study of Opinion Makers* (1969).

The table shows that both manual and non-manual workers' children were represented more than proportional to the population as a whole, though the share of opinion makers with non-manual occupations (39·2 per cent) was double its proportion of the total population (18·9 per cent). Children born in peasants' families were underrepresented: they constituted 49·2 per cent of the total population but only 22·1 per cent of the opinion makers. The elite sectors show interesting differences in the social origins of members: the political and economic elites are drawn largely from the manual and agricultural workers (69·2 per cent of the legislators, 68·4 per cent of the political and 71·6 per cent of the economic leaders), whereas the leaders in the mass media (journalists 50·4 per cent) and 'intellectual' sector (58·6 per cent) are predominantly *non-manual*, and 40 per cent of administrators also come from a non-manual background. Of course, the Yugoslav data relating to a period only twenty-four years after the assumption of power by the Communists, reflect the political priorities and ascribed promotion of manual and agricultural workers during the early years of power.

A Polish study of full-time executives in local government (chairman, vice-chairman and secretary) distinguishes between their social origin and their career paths. Of the total surveyed (7576 men), 93·9 per cent were of manual worker (33·1 per cent) and peasant (60·8 per cent) origin; only 5 per cent had parents who were non-manual workers. When one considers the intra-generational mobility, one sees that in fact the majority of these men actually began employment in *non-manual* work. The socio-occupational group by their first employment was non-manual for 56·7 per cent of the executives (32·1 per cent had been administrative or office workers); 16·3 per cent had had manual industrial first jobs and only 4·6 per cent had begun work in manual agricultural labour (Zagorski, 1970, pp. 14–15). As these are the men from whom the future political elites are recruited, one can expect that the number of leaders who have had to work with their hands will decline.

We might conclude this section by saying that while upward

social mobility (see p. 29) has undoubtedly been very great in state-socialist societies in recent years, it has been largely a result of industrialization and the creation of many new positions, both manual and non-manual. There have also been in operation factors which seem to limit downward inter-generational mobility. Children from urban areas and from the higher professional and other non-manual families have not only better access to cultural facilities but also higher aspirations. Family background makes more 'educable' the children of parents with higher educational and professional attainment. The educational sub-system may have values at variance with those of the political elite's system of values. The latter may stress equality of educational opportunity, but the educational system itself tends to seek to produce as efficiently as possible properly skilled and motivated man-power; and to do this it selects students who will benefit most from the use of its scarce resources. Hence the modern educational system, whose main function it is to train and to allocate labour, has direct selective effects on the system of social stratification. While a lower proportion of children from manual backgrounds compared to non-manuals aspire to higher education, there is nevertheless a considerable absolute number who do so and who find their desires frustrated by the superior educational performance of the non-manual employees' children. While these tendencies may be counteracted to some extent by unstreamed comprehensive education, such measures cannot fully overcome the inequalities of opportunity created by differences in family milieux. We may conclude then that with the greater economic maturity and political stability of the kind of societies under consideration there is a tendency for the higher social strata to be self recruiting. In the absence of any significant increase in the rate of industrial development or significant political changes in state socialist societies, one might expect the pattern of social stratification to become more stable and the amount of upward mobility to decline.

At the same time, one cannot realistically assume that the many strata forming 'the intelligentsia' are a unitary social group. Though it may be conceded that such strata are accorded certain privileges – for they have high income, they are often in control of other men and their jobs give them high status – they are not a homogeneous category. In particular the cultural and technical intelligentsia is said to be subject to *political* control: writers, for instance, are occasionally imprisoned, social scientists' research is often not published and scientists' projects may be determined by the government. Therefore, it is important to discuss separately the social background of the political elites, the top men in the Communist Party and ministerial apparatus, to see from which levels of society they originate and whether they are a self-perpetuating group.

Political recruitment

The Communist Party of the Soviet Union (and analogous parties in Eastern Europe) which may be said to perform the function of aggregating political interests, is widely believed to be the dominant political institution in Soviet society. There are two aspects of this crucial organization to be considered in the present context: firstly, the social composition of the party, and secondly, the 'placement' role of the party in respect of positions in other institutions.

There can be no doubt that the social grouping of the non-manual employees predominates among the membership of the CPSU (Table 21). Examination of the data shows that the non-manual strata are the largest single group in the membership of the party: they constituted 50·9 per cent in 1956, 45·4 per cent in 1968 and 44·8 per cent in 1971. This situation is paralleled in Poland where in 1966 non-manual workers accounted for 42·6 per cent of the membership of the Polish United Workers Party (PUWP), the share of manual workers was 40·2 per cent, and peasants 11·7. Put in a different way, of the occupationally active population, 29·8 per cent of non-manual workers, 12·2 per cent of manual workers and only 3·8 per cent of peasants were members of the PUWP (Sadowski, 1968, pp. 93–4).[4] The higher grades of non-manual workers, particularly scientists and researchers, are likely to be

4. On Yugoslavia, Hungary and Czechoslovakia, see Parkin (1969).

Table 21

Social Structure of USSR (Official figures) and Social
Composition of CPSU

Social structure of USSR			Party composition	
	1959 %	1968 %	1956 %	1968 %
Manual and non-manual workers	68·3	77·7	82·9	84·2
Of which: manual	48·2	54·0*	32·0	38·8
non-manual	20·1	23·7*	50·9	45·4
Collective farm peasants	31·4	22·3	17·1	15·8
	100·0	100·0	100·0	100·0

*Estimate, not given in sources

Sources: Semenov (1964, p. 258). Party composition 1968: *KPSS*
(1969, p. 9). Tsentral'noe (1969, p. 35). In 1968 the total number of
employed manual and non-manual workers was 85·1 millions – non-
manual being 29·9 million (pp. 35, 547). See also p. 25. In 1971 9 per cent
of the adult population were party members; 40 per cent were classified
as manual, 45 per cent as non-manual, and 15 per cent as collective
farmers (*Pravda*, 31 March 1971).

party members[5] and many statistics have been collected to
show the extent of party 'saturation' of these kinds of posts.
A study of the party background of Soviet local government
deputies found the following steep graduation of party
membership according to occupation: factory directors 99 per
cent, 'sub-directional management' 51 per cent, foremen and
other junior supervisory posts 38 per cent, specialists lacking
administrative powers 27 per cent, workers 18 per cent. These
figures, of course, relate to the more politically inclined
personnel who also take part in local government. General
figures available for some major professional groups show
that in 1964, 25 per cent of teachers were party members and
that among doctors and engineers the membership ran at 22

5. In the USSR, party groups in scientific institutions in 1965 were
eighty-five strong on average – larger than those in industrial enterprises ('KPSS v tsifrakh').

per cent and 42 per cent respectively (Rigby, 1968. p. 433–9)
Thus the CPSU is not socially representative of the population of the USSR: the non-manual strata, particularly the
executive and professional occupations, are overrepresented
and the collective farm peasantry are underweighted. The
manual working-class also has relatively fewer party members
than its share of the total population.

At the level of the party elite this unrepresentativeness is
even more pronounced. For example, at the Twenty-Third
Congress in 1966, the 'top-level bureaucracy' made up 2·1 per
cent of total party members, but it accounted for 40 per cent
of the delegates to the Congress and 81·1 per cent of the full
members of the Central Committee (Meissner, 1966). In 1966,
the Central Committee of the party had 195 full members and
165 candidate members: and 91 per cent of the full members
and 86·5 per cent of the candidates had had higher education.
Of the total (members and candidates together), 42 per cent
were men engaged full-time in the party apparatus, 28 per
cent were in the apparatus of government, 14 per cent were
army officers, diplomats and police chiefs, and about 12 per
cent were drawn from the other sundry jobs. The last group
included fifteen outstanding workers, eight trade-union leaders, seven members of the Academies of Sciences, five directors
of large industrial enterprises, four leaders of associations of
creative writers and three persons from the Komsomol (Voritsyn, 1969; Gehlen, 1969, pp. 42–9). The party elite, therefore,
is largely composed of top officials from the party and governmental bureaucracies. This does not mean of course that such
officials have not begun their careers from lowly backgrounds.
Indeed, analysis of the social origins of these men shows that
most had working class or peasant backgrounds. Of the full
members of the Central Committee, 27 per cent were the
children of manual workers, 35 per cent claimed peasant
origin, 12 per cent non-manual, and 26 per cent were not
defined. Even if all of the last group originated from the non-
manual strata, the data would not indicate that they yet form a
hereditary class or ruling group. This becomes even clearer
if we consider the membership of the politbureau/presidium
of the party. Of the twenty-seven members of this body

between 1917 and 1951, eight were the sons of manual workers, seven originated from the peasantry, seven had a non-manual background and five were of unknown social origin (Schneller, 1966, p. 105). Comparing these data with the social origins of the members of the politbureau between 1966 and 1971 we may conclude that there has been very little change.[6] But many of these political activists became communists during the early days of Soviet power (the average age of the Politbureau in 1971 was sixty-three years) and any tendencies towards a more hereditary system may become clearer with the advent of a new generation of Soviet leaders.[7]

Let us now turn to consider the extent to which the party allocates men to other positions in various parts of Soviet society, for in this way it may have considerable power to shape the pattern of social mobility. We have seen in earlier chapters that one of the most important changes which limited the ascription of position was the nationalization of property, which meant the elimination of inheritance of substantial wealth, and of private ownership of the means of production. But such ownership relations are not unique determinants of status, power and privilege. We have seen that after the October Revolution, administrative mechanisms allocated privilege to previously deprived classes. Then as now the Communist Party selected and allocated personnel to all positions of power in Russia by making appointments and elections to higher positions in state socialist societies subject to 'party control'. In practice the cadres (or personnel) department of the party's secretariat exercises the placement function. It may actively suggest individuals for certain positions and it may also veto the appointments made by the

6. The social origins of twenty-one full and candidate members were: manual working class nine, peasantry seven, non-manual workers four, unknown one.

7. A study of 139 regional party first secretaries in 1966 shows that 36 per cent had peasant origins, 18 per cent manual worker, and 5 per cent non-manual backgrounds. (I would like to thank Mr Peter Frank for putting these figures at my disposal.) These figures are inconclusive, however, because the origins of 41 per cent of the sample were not known and the future political elite could possibly be promoted from a stratum of this group.

'cadres' departments of other institutions. In view of this practice, some writers have argued that party administrative selection in state-socialist societies replaces the kind of ascription on the basis of ownership which occurs at the highest levels of capitalist societies.

Few comprehensive data are available to us on the actual operation of the secretariat in its placement function. Party control is exercised in two ways: by influencing elections to the Communist Party, the Soviets (parliaments) and trade unions; and by sanctioning appointments to executive posts in organizations (offices, factories, the army, etc.) which come under the various government ministries. Little empirical research is available on the extent of this process of social selection. Churchward has estimated that 35 per cent of all administrative positions involving 600,000 posts are subject to party control (1968, p. 206). However, just what constitutes 'control' is very obscure. It is often asserted that the party penetrates other structures so that:

party career divisions within both the state bureaucracy and the party bureaucracy are much more significant than the division between these bureaucracies. In fact, there is such a high degree of interchange between the middle levels of the state and party bureaucracies that it is impossible to look upon these organizations as separate elite segments. Moreover, the principal line officials of both state and party are so closely associated by both training and career as to constitute a single body (Armstrong, 1959, p. 144).

Recent studies of the career paths of party secretaries and factory directors would suggest, however, that the lines between party and governmental careers are now more firmly drawn. Stewart's study (1968) of a sample of 208 party secretaries who held their positions between 1950 and 1966 shows that *prior to* becoming officials they had worked in a variety of occupations. The following figures show the limited extent to which they were transferred, as might be generalist administrators, to important positions in the state apparatus. Of the careers studied of 202 local first secretaries, Stewart shows that only four were 'promoted' to positions in the federal government apparatus,[8] and thirty-one were 'transferred' to similar positions in the republican government apparatus. On the other hand, sixty-four were promoted to higher positions in the party apparatus. Another study by Hough of the chairmen appointed in 1957 to the Regional Economic Councils (*sovnarkhozy*) shows that out of a sample of ninety-seven men (about whom biographical data were collected) only six had previously been party officials, and the remainder had been recruited from senior administrators and executives in government service. Also, in considering the background of the directors of important plants, Hough found that all but one had had an engineering background – and forty-six out of forty-eight biographies showed that they were graduate engineers. Moreover, these men had risen within the industrial hierarchies; in 1958 they were men in their late forties or early fifties 'with three decades of experience in industrial management' (1969, pp. 58–9, 62)

The work of Stewart and Hough then modifies considerably Armstrong's view, stated above, that party and state bureaucracies might be considered as a single body. But perhaps even more crucial than interchange at the middle and regional levels of administration is the social background and career paths of the ministers who guide the economy of the USSR to whom we shall now turn.

The Council of Ministers elected in 1966 was made up of a chairman, two vice-chairmen, forty-seven ministers, fourteen chairmen of various committees and fifteen chairmen of the Councils of Ministers of Union Republics. The biographical data collected on the forty-seven ministers are shown on Table 22. The social origin of the ministers shows that twenty-seven out of forty were known to have come from peasant and manual-worker families. It is doubtful whether any of the seven who did not give their social origin came from these strata and it is probable that they withheld information (such as bourgeois background) which may have made them politically less acceptable. Also, the categorization 'peasant'

8. i.e. as chairman or deputy chairman USSR Council of Ministers and USSR minister or deputy minister.

Table 22

Social Background of Ministers in U S S R Council of Ministers (1966)

Social origin		
Peasants		11
Workers		16
Non-manual		13
of which: teachers	4	
lower clerical (*sluzhashchie*)	7	
agronomist	1	
physician	1	
Not given		7
		47

Education	
Higher	45
Incomplete higher	1
Not stated	1
	47

Age on joining Party	
23–25	19
26–30	19
Over 30	9
	47

Career paths	
Having career in government organizations	37
Having career in Party, *Komsomol*, Trade Union and government organizations	10
	47

Source: Based on biographies in *Deputaty verkhovnogo soveta SSSR* (1966).

or 'worker' is a very general one and it is even possible that some 'peasant' fathers may have been actually occupied for a part of their lives in non-manual jobs. Therefore, one might conclude that between a third and a half of the ministers came from non-manual backgrounds. Even so, the data would not substantiate the conclusion that the upper professional or even non-manual groups in general were 'inheriting' the top governmental positions. On the other hand, the educational level of the ministers is very high; all but two are known to have completed higher education and, what is more, in most cases this was in their ministerial profession. Now let us consider how far these men were recruited from party activists.

Distinguishing simply between those who had worked in government institutions and those who had worked in party/ *komsomol*, trade union *and* government institutions, we see from their career paths that nearly four-fifths had had a career exclusively in government institutions. Even of the ten who had held posts outside (in party, *komsomol* or union) three had been *komsomol* officials only during an early part of their career and had subsequently made a full-time career in government service. Also, since 1950, only five had switched between higher party and government jobs.

We might fairly confidently conclude that the heads of the Soviet ministerial system are career industrialists and that the party in current practice does not very often transfer its own men to the higher levels of government service. The evidence indicates that Soviet ministers are specialists and have spent most of their working lives in their own ministry. While it is too sweeping a statement to say that a rigid structural differentiation takes place between party and government administration, the evidence cited above leads us to conclude that there is a tendency to internal recruitment within the party and ministerial hierarchies.

It is outside the scope of this short book to consider in detail the extent of political conflict between the various elites in state-socialist society.[9] But the evidence presented above

9. The points which follow have been dealt with at greater length in Lane (1970, chs. 7 and 8).

suggests that the Communist Party does not ascribe positions in governmental institutions as a reward for political activity, though at the lower and middle levels of the hierarchy it still has a certain amount of patronage at its disposal. Also appointment to managerial and scientific positions is determined by education and qualifications; it is meritocratic rather than ascribed by the party authorities. Nevertheless, one of the main cleavages in state socialist society is between those groups whose authority lies in the Communist Party (for example, party secretaries) and others whose position is technocratic and professional.[10] We saw earlier in this chapter that with the maturity of the state-socialist system, the social structure becomes less flexible and more rigidly stratified with benefits and advantages accruing to the professional, executive and technical groups. Party activists believing in classlessness and equality may articulate policies through the party *apparat* which seek to redress the balance of the power between them and such groups (Feldmesser, 1967, pp. 527–33). Such a cleavage between party *apparatchiks* and ideologists, on the one side, and professionals and technical specialists, on the other, is a dynamic factor in the internal politics of state-socialist society. The development of a 'market' form of economy will obviously enhance the power of the technocrats and professionals and at the same time reduce the influence of purely party functionaries. The effects of a 'market' structure will probably be to increase salary differentials at the expense of the manual working-class and future politics in state-socialist society might see a strengthening of the links between the party *apparatchiks* and the manual working-class in their opposition to the technocratic and professional groupings.

10. Parkin, in discussing Poland, Hungary, Czechoslovakia and Yugoslavia, has noted the 'quite sharp antagonisms ... between the younger generation of graduates and technocrats on the one hand and the older party veterans and partisans on the other ... In Czechoslovakia ... opposition to the economic reforms came from factory managers whose appointment owed more to their politics and proletarian origins than to their technical abilities' (1969, pp. 365-7).

6 Conclusions

In the foregoing chapters we have seen that the Bolshevik Revolution succeeded in changing the fundamental relations of power and property but that it has not subsequently created a society ensuring the equality of men, one in which social stratification is absent. There are four reasons why social inequality persists in the USSR and in states modelled on her; it has been perpetuated firstly, by property relations, secondly, by the system of political power, thirdly, by the division of labour and fourthly, by the human nuclear family. Let us consider each and then turn to outline the major social cleavages in state-socialist society.

The concept of class with which Marx, Lenin and Stalin are associated takes as its starting point the relations of social groups to the ownership of the means of production. Whereas the inalienable right of man to possess private property was proclaimed by the French Revolution, the Russian Revolution of October 1917 sought to destroy the human bondage to private property. In both revolutions class rights played a large and important part – they were a catalyst of the desires for social change of particular social groups. After the Bolshevik Revolution, the concept of class struggle became a dominating factor in the transformation of Russia. The ideology of historical materialism in which class rights prominently figured severely limited the possibilities of social action which were open to Russia's leaders and it became the basis of a value system on which the actual structure of social relations in the USSR and other East European societies has been built and judged. The incumbents of power in the USSR, those who defend it as a socialist society, are committed to a view of the world which gives to the private ownership of property primacy in the determination of social relations. But ownership has both legal and social connotations. In a legal sense it gives exclusive rights to the possessor of an object to dispose of it or enjoy it. But the rules or legal charter of a society may not coincide with actual social relations. Certain groups (for example, government ministers and their subordinates such as factory directors) may in fact have certain rights over objects which are not given legal recognition, and this makes formal legal interpretations unrealistic. Hence many writers, and not only the 'official' Soviet ones, have considered ownership and the classes arising from it in a mechanical way. While large-scale *private* property has been largely abolished, property is not owned in common in state-socialist societies. In addition to private ownership in agriculture (the produce of personal plots), the notion of property is perpetuated by institutional control of wealth (for example by the state bank, ministries and institutions). These factors not only influence the individual's consciousness of property but give rights and privileges to those who are able to control property. The implications of such ownership forms are twofold. On the one hand, the incumbents of power positions (those with authority) do not form an ownership class which can be understood in classical Marxist terms. Assets are not disposed of through families in state-socialist societies. Government ministers and directors of factories do not pass on rights over ministries or factories to their sons as may capitalists in capitalist societies. Also, those with control over property giving them privileges in the distribution of rewards are not conscious of their property rights and therefore they do not form a ruling class as defined by Marx. This difference represents a break between the system of stratification in Western advanced capitalist societies and those of the Soviet type. On the other hand, societies arranged on the model of the USSR are not 'socialist' in the way in which classical Marxists conceived of such a social system. A necessary condition for a socialist type of society is not only the abolition of proprietory classes, but also the development of productive forces to a stage higher than that allowed by the fetters of capitalist property relations. However, most of the societies of Eastern Europe considered have been characterized by a relatively underdeveloped industrial structure, being at the time of the Communist seizure of power nowhere near the level of that of the advanced states of Western Europe and the USA. Thus it is not surprising that with the development of these states the pattern of social relations which they exhibit is not in general qualitatively different from that of capitalist societies and is unlikely to be so until the capacity of the productive forces has surpassed those of the advanced capitalist societies of the West. Under the conditions inherited by the Communists in Eastern Europe, the bourgeoisie's traditional task of capital formation involving urbanization and industrialization became that of the state which shaped to some extent the particular pattern of social stratification.

We have seen that the state had an impact on the group structure of East European societies: put simply, political power did not grow out of the group structure, it created a group structure. The predominantly agrarian societies of Eastern Europe have been industrialized by the political elites, and from such processes have followed changes in the number and size of occupational groups and in the distribution of income. This social transformation function of the state must not be exaggerated. It is *not* true to say that '. . . the system of inequality that we call social stratification is only a secondary consequence of the social structure of power' (Dahrendorf, 1969, p. 38). Certain forms of social inequality are independent of, rather than determined by, the system of political power. Those with the power to coerce other men (say party officials or bureaucrats) do not always have high evaluation in terms of honour. The ideology which such men concoct to justify their privilege and that of other social strata is insufficient to define the actual system of social relations. The 'official charter' describes the urban working class as the legitimate bearer of socialist virtue and power but in practice the working class is stratified. The urban intelligentsia occupy positions of power (in the party and government) and those of social honour (the professions) whereas the manual working class has much less power and honour. Study of the changing pattern of income differentials brings out the ways political ideological goals have been modified when under stress from adaptive economic pressures. The early policies of the Communist Party which aimed at levelling out incomes generally have not been long lasting because the constraints of economic and technical efficiency have required wider differentials. The evidence presented in this text showing similarities between capitalist and state-socialist societies concerning differential access to education, and the evaluation of the status or occupations, seems overwhelming and conclusive. These facts suggest that the political elites have been unable in some respects to shape the system of social stratification to their own specifications, and that they have been confronted with other social forces and institutions which have a certain autonomy. While the *origins* of the system of social stratification are to be found in the political order, after a revolutionary change many patterns of inequality come to approximate to the social stratification systems of other industrial societies. Particularly important in this respect are the impact of the division of labour and the functions performed by the family.

Social relations in modern industrial society are specialized and specific; there is a highly developed division of labour. The economic division of labour gives some men the creative tasks, those of planning and ordering the work of others; but the majority do the intellectually less exacting and routine jobs. The occupations of men profoundly influence the esteem in which other men hold them and affect the way of life they follow. The intrinsic satisfaction of creative and executive jobs is greater than that of unskilled. The job itself develops or hinders other individual capacities: those with creative positions are able to exploit their intelligence, they become skilled in manipulating symbols, machines and other men. They form social groups and mix with others of a similar intellectual background. Similarly, the occupation of the unskilled also influences their ranking in terms of power and honour. Hence, as long as the economic organization of society calls for the division of labour, status differentials are likely to continue.

Two points may be made here about the practical possibilities of creating an equalitarian society. Firstly, one may reject the argument of those egalitarians who claim that all jobs are equally 'necessary' in a society and that therefore all should be equal in status. While any job may be 'necessary' if it has a social purpose, not all jobs may be performed equally well by each individual and some form of role differentiation is necessary to promote the effective use of resources through technical efficiency. Educational systems are structures whose *raison d'être* is to train some men for more complicated and specialized tasks and others to accept the less demanding and more routine. The former are given a near monopoly of certain skills and those with no skill or little skill are in a weak competitive position whereas the skilled can much more easily perform unskilled jobs. At any given time, therefore, the indispensibility of the highly skilled, as they are more difficult to substitute is greater than that of the unskilled. Secondly, those with intellectual skills have control over political power, they are able to manipulate symbols and to coin ideologies which justify their privileges. To some extent they may be able to maintain privileges which are quite unrelated to their scarcity and to manipulate other men to believe that their privileges are necessary for the society to function properly. The division of labour then has a certain 'objective' hierarchy built into it and also has a self-justifying mechanism. Even if the view that all contribute equally to the maintenance of a system is over-simple, the ability of the privileged groups to appropriate more than an equal share of the social product and to secure the compliance of the underprivileged to their superiority are based on the division of labour and will continue until it is no longer necessary. Thus attempts to 'introduce equality' by influencing social norms through the educational system are likely to have only limited effect unless accompanied by significant changes in the economic system (the mode of production).

The fourth source of inequality in state-socialist society

defined at the beginning of the chapter is the nuclear family as an institution. Parents have an occupational role and status in society which under present arrangements significantly influences their children's access to the culture of that society. The inheritance of wealth has been restricted by the structural form of state-socialist society and has had the effect of making social position more dependent on achievement rather than ascription by family origin. But to a very great extent access to education, to the stock of knowledge of how the system works and to basic social and intellectual skills is still inherited through the family circle, thereby thwarting the equalitarian plans pursued by revolutionary leaders. During the periods of rapid industrialization and social change which characterized the early period of communist power in state-socialist society, the family was weakened and the social structure was in flux. After this period, and with the consolidation of communist rule, the family has been strengthened and there has been a tendency to a less flexible system of social stratification. There are two reasons for the persistence of the nuclear family in a form similar to that of the capitalist West First, it is an institution through which individuals may satisfy their own emotional demands: to give and to receive affection, to gratify their sexual urges. It is also a mechanism which helps to integrate the social order. It ensures the care, maintenance and socialization of children and in so doing, it does not infringe upon the rights of the privileged. Thus the incumbents of positions of power and privilege find it useful both in their own interest and in the interest of society as a whole to strengthen the family. At the same time, the family perpetuates other attitudes which may be at variance with the values of the elites. For instance, prejudice about the inferiority of woman and her 'proper' roles and about national and ethnic groups is passed on in the socialization process which takes place in the family.

The major social cleavages in state-socialist society are threefold. First, there are differences between the working class (both manual and non-manual) and the peasantry. The latter occupies an inferior position when compared to the working class in terms of income, access to power (party) and social honour. Such differences are accounted for by the peasantry's greater attachment to private property and also by the peculiar values of Eastern European societies where peasants have historically constituted the most under-privileged and least honoured stratum. Secondly, there is a cleavage between manual and non-manual labour. While income differentials sometimes mask such differences, there is a fairly well crystallized division between those who work mainly with their hands and those who use their brains. This cleavage is much less distinct on the borderline between unskilled non-manual and skilled manual, but is more definite at the upper levels between the 'socialist intelligentsia' with higher educational qualifications and the rest of the manual strata. This group is differentiated by high social honour, high income, more 'cultured' forms of consumption and by patterns of friendship and marriages. In the period of rapid industrialization and political change it has been characterized by much recruitment from the manual strata, but with the slow-down of economic growth and with the greater stability of the political system, this feature will probably become less distinctive and will give way to internal regeneration. The third main cleavage in state-socialist society is between the party elite which has its privilege grounded in political power and the technocratic and professional groups whose rights are based on technical and administrative knowledge. The ideals and values of socialist revolution have been associated with the former, but the party's role in an industrial society has atrophied. A state-socialist society is above all a technical-administrative society, where man's social position is increasingly determined by education, qualifications and technical-administrative performance. The purely party functionaries are outside this stratum, their skills have traditionally been based on political qualities (cunning, demagogy) and such political skills still give them political power, but this is restricted by the demands and integrity of the cultural, technical and administrative elites. While there is a rivalry for the institutionalization of power, the elites also have a certain identity of interests to maintain their privileges against the non-elites. This balance is sometimes upset, as it was in Czechoslovakia when one element of the elite (the technical and cultural intelligentsia) utilized the non-elite to try to secure for itself greater power at the expense of another elite element (the party bureaucrats). The social foundation of politics in state socialist society then is neither one of ownership classes in the Marxist sense, nor of a ruling elite and fragmented mass as postulated by the theorists of totalitarianism. It is one of elites which to some extent are in conflict between themselves but are also subject to pressures arising from the non-elite.

We may conclude by saying that the system of social stratification in state-socialist society has peculiar features distinguishing it from those of advanced capitalist states. The limited individual *private* inheritance of wealth has eliminated ownership classes as known in capitalist societies, but it has put a premium on achievement as a mode by which inequality has been maintained and thus has given rise to institutional control over wealth enabling some men to have rights over property which others are denied. The ideology of state-socialist society has, perhaps marginally, enhanced the status of the workers as a social group, the extent of income differentials has been minimized and sex differences have been reduced. But inequality is a characteristic of state-socialist society as it is of the capitalist: there is inequality of control over wealth, inequality of political power, inequality of income and inequality of status. The origins of such social stratification lie in differential control of property, in the role structure created by the division of labour, sanctioned by the educational system and perpetuated by the family. Such structural features give rise to a hierarchy in which some groups of men have power, prestige and privilege while others lack them. Politically, and not without internal conflict, the privileged acquire the means to help maintain and to justify ideologically their privilege. Though social equality is a worthy ideal, the recent history of state-socialist society shows that it cannot be attained by the wishes of men independently of the economic structure of society. 'Men make their own history, but they do not make it under circumstances chosen by themselves but under circumstances directly encountered, given and transmitted from the past' (Marx, 1958a, p. 247). Until such circumstances make differential ownership and control of property, the division of labour and the socializing influence of the nuclear family no longer necessary for the flourishing of industrial society, social inequality will remain a characteristic of the relations between men.

Appendix

Occupational hierarchies according to education, authority, income and prestige in Poland.

	Ranking by			
	Education	Authority	Income	Prestige
Physicians and dentists p	1	7	2	4
Engineers and architects p	2	2	1	3
Natural-science professionals, mathematicians and physicists p	3	4	16	5
Lawyers and economists p	4	3	6	6·5
Teachers p	5	5·5	15	2
Managers of politico-economic life p	6	1	4	8
Liberal-art professionals and creative artists p	7	5·5	12	1
Technicians in industry t	8·5	8·5	7	11
Medium-level medical assistants t	8·5	17·5	25	6·5
Laboratory assistants t	10	10	14	10
Office employees in public administration o	11	17·5	10	26·5
Office employees in social-services institutions o	12	11·5	27	25
Office employees in industry and construction o	13	8·5	9	19
Office employees in the sector of service o	14	11·5	19	20
Technicians in trade t	15	14·4	8	12
Office employees in trade o	16	14·5	21	26·5
Foremen f	17	13	11	13

	Ranking by			
	Edu-cation	Auth-ority	Income	Prestige
Master workers f	18	16	17	18
Shopkeepers and tradesmen c	19	23	3	31·5
Salesmen and distributors s	20·5	24	32	22
Service-workers	20·5	21	22	35
Artisans – owners of work-shops c	22	18·5	5	23·5
Artisans – members of cooperatives c	23	22	18	21
Drivers and conductors s	24	18·5	23	17·5
Steel workers and lathe operators w_1	25·5	26	20	9
Skilled workers in transport w_1	25·5	28·5	33	28
Homeworkers c	27	25	13	31·5
Skilled workers in the sector of service w_1	28	27	28	14
Semi-skilled workers in heavy industry w_2	29	35·5	26	23·5
Skilled workers in construction w_1	30	28·5	29	16
Skilled workers in light industry w_1	31	30	24	15
Semi-skilled workers in construction w_2	32	35·5	38	33
Semi-skilled workers in transport w_2	33	35·5	36	35
Semi-skilled workers in the sector of service w_2	35	35·5	34	29
Unskilled workers in heavy industry w_3	35	35·5	30	38
Semi-skilled workers in light industry w_2	35	35·5	31	30
Unskilled workers in the sector of service w_3	37	35·5	37	36
Unskilled workers in heavy industry w_3	38	35·5	39	39

| | Ranking by | | | |
	Education	Authority	Income	Prestige
Unskilled workers in construction w_3	39	35·5	35	40
Unskilled workers in transport w_3	40	35·5	40	37

p – professionals; t – technicians; o – office employees;
f – foremen; s – service workers; c – craftsmen;
w_1 – skilled workers; w_2 – semi-skilled workers;
w_3 – unskilled workers.

Source: Slomczynski (1970, pp. 33–4).

References

Aganbegyan, A. G., Osipov, G. V., and Shubkin. V. N. (1966) *Kolichestvennye metody v sotsiologii*, Moscow.

Andreyuk, G. P. (1966), 'Vydvizhenchestvo i ego rol' v formirovanii intelligentsii (1921–32 gg.)', *Iz istorii sovetskoy intelligentsii*, Moscow.

Arendt, H. (1958), *The Origins of Totalitarianism*, World Publishing Company.

Armstrong, J. A. (1959), *The Soviet Bureaucratic Elite: A Case Study of the Ukranian Apparatus*, Praeger.

Aron, R. (1950), 'Social structure and ruling class,' (pt 1) *Brit. J. Sociol.*, vol. 1 (pt 2) vol. 1, no. 2.

Arutyunyan, Yu. V. (1969), 'Konkretno-sotsiologicheskoe issledovanie natsional'nykh otnosheniy' *Voprosy filosofii*, no. 12.

Aspaturian, V. V. (1968), 'The non-Russian nationalities' in A. Kassof (ed.), *Prospects for Soviet Society*, Pall Mall Press.

Bain, G. S. (1970), *The Growth of White-Collar Unionism*, Oxford University Press.

Barber, B. (1957), *Social Stratification*, Harcourt, Brace & World.

Baykov, A. (1947), *The Development of the Soviet Economic System: An Essay on the Experience of Planning in the USSR*, Cambridge University Press.

Bendix, R., and Lipset, S. M. (1959), *Social Mobility in Industrial Society*, University of California Press.

Bergson, A. (1944), *The Structure of Soviet Wages, A Study in Socialist Economics*, Harvard University Press.

Béteille, A. (ed.) (1969), *Social Inequality*, Penguin.

Bialer, S. (1966), *Soviet Political Elite: Concept, Sample, Case Study*, Columbia University: Ph.D. Dissertation.

Bienstock, G., Schwarz, S. M., and Yugow, A. (1948), *Management in Russian Industry and Agriculture*, Cornell University Press.

Bilinsky, J. (1967), 'The rulers and the ruled', *Problems of Communism*, vol. 16, no. 5. pp. 16–26.

Blumberg, P. (1968), *Industrial Democracy: The Sociology of Participation*, Constable.

Bolgov, A. V. (1962), 'Preodolenie sushchestvennykh razlichiy mezhdu gorodom i derevney', *Ot sotsializma k kommunizmu*, Moscow.

BOTTOMORE, T. B. (1965), *Classes in Modern Society*, Allen & Unwin.

BRZEZINSKI, Z., and HUNTINGTON, S. P. (1964), *Political Power: USA/USSR*, Chatto & Windus.

BUBNOV, A. (1930), 'VKP (B)'*Bol'shaya Sovetskaya Entsiklopediya*, vol. 11, Moscow.

BURNHAM, J. (1941), *The Managerial Revolution*, Indiana University Press; Penguin, 1945.

CARR, E. H. (1950), *The Bolshevik Revolution 1917–23*, vol. 1, Macmillan; Penguin, 1966.

CHARLTON, K. (1968), 'Polytechnical Education', *International Rev. of Educ.*, vol. 14, no. 1.

CHURCHWARD, L. G. (1968), 'Bureaucracy – USA: USSR' *Co-existence*, vol. V, no. 2, pp. 201–9.

CLIFF, T. (1964), *Russia: A Marxist Analysis*, Socialist Review Publishers.

COHN-BENDIT, G. and D. (1969), *Obsolete Communism: The Left-Wing Alternative*, Penguin.

The Constitution of the USSR (1969), Moscow, Progress Publishers.

CONQUEST, R. (1967), *Soviet Nationalities Policy in Practice*, Bodley Head.

CROSLAND, C. A. R. (1956), *The Future of Socialism*, Cape.

DAHRENDORF, R. (1969), 'On the origin of inequality among men', in A. Béteille (ed.), *Social Inequality*, Penguin.

Deputaty verkhovnogo soveta SSSR (1966), Moscow.

DEWAR, M. (1962), 'Labour and wage reforms in the USSR', *Studies in the Soviet Union* (Munich), vol. 3, no. 3.

DE WITT, N. (1961), *Educational and Professional Manpower in the USSR*, National Research Council.

DJILAS, M. (1966), *The New Class, an Analysis of the Communist System*, Allen & Unwin.

DODGE, N. T. (1966), *Women in the Soviet Economy*, Johns Hopkins University Press.

DROBIZHEV, V. Z. (1961), 'Rol' rabochego klassa SSSR v formirovanii komandnykh kadrov sotsialisticheskoy promyshlennosti (1917–1936)', *Istoriya SSSR*, 1961, no. 4, pp. 55–75.

Dukhovoe razvitie lichnosti 1967, Sverdlovsk.

ELMEEV, V. YA., *et al.* (1965), *Kommunizm i preodolenie razdeleniya mezhdu umstvennym i fizicheskim trudom*, Leningrad.

ENGELS, F. (1951), 'The origins of the family, private property and the state', in *Marx–Engels, Selected Works*, vol. 2, Moscow.

FELDMESSER, R. A. (1957), 'Social status and access to higher education', *Harvard Educ. Rev.*, vol. 27, no. 2.

FELDMESSER, R. A. (1966), 'Towards the classless society?' in R. Bendix and S. M. Lipset (eds.), *Class, Status and Power*, Routledge & Kegan Paul.

FERGE, S. (1966), *Volosag*, Budapest.

FOGARTY, M. P., RAPOPORT, R., and RAPOPORT, R. N. (1971), *Sex, Career and Family*, Allen & Unwin.

FRIEDRICH, C. J. and BRZEZINSKI, Z. K. (1966), *Totalitarian Dictatorship and Autocracy*, Praeger.

GEHLEN, M. P. (1969), *The Communist Party of the Soviet Union*, Indiana University Press.

GERSCHENKRON, A. (1947), 'The rate of industrial growth in Russia since 1885', *J. Econ. Hist.*, vol. 7 (Supplement), pp. 144–74.

GLEZERMAN, G. (1968), 'Sotsial'naya struktura sotsialisticheskogo obshchestva', *Kommunist*, no. 13, pp. 28–39. Also in *Soviet News* (London), 12 November 1968.

GLOWACKI, W. (1959), 'Pracownicy "Kasprzaka" o zarobkach', in *Zycie Gospodarcze*, no. 14, 5 April 1959.

GOLDTHORPE, J. H. (1967), 'Social stratification in industrial society', in R. Bendix and S. M. Lipset (eds.), *Class, Status and Power: Social Stratification in Comparative Perspective*, Routledge & Kegan Paul, pp. 648–59.

GOLDTHORPE, J. H. *et al.* (1969), *The Affluent Worker in the Class Structure* vol. 3, Cambridge University Press.

GURYANOV, S. T. (1966), 'Vertical mobility of employees in an enterprise', in G. V. Osipov (ed.) *Industry and Labour in the USSR*, Tavistock.

HOBSBAWM, E. J. (1968), *Industry and Empire*, Weidenfeld & Nicolson, Penguin, 1969.

HOUGH, J. F. (1969), *The Soviet Prefects: The Local Party Organs in Industrial Decision-Making*, Harvard University Press.

HUNGARIAN CENTRAL STATISTICAL OFFICE (1967), *Social Stratification in Hungary*, Budapest.

INKELES, A., and ROSSI, P. H. (1956), 'National comparisons of occupational prestige', *Amer. J. Socio.*, vol. 61, no. 4, pp. 329–39.

International Study of Opinion Makers (1969) (Yugoslav Section). Sponsored by Columbia University. Duplicated paper; London School of Economics and Political Science.

IOVCHUK, M. T., KOGAN, L., and RUTKEVICH, M. N. (1962), 'Pod'em kul' turnotekhnicheskogo urovnya rabochego klassa i ego rol' v soedinenii fizicheskogo i umstvennogo truda v SSSR', *Ot sotsializma k kommunizmu*, Moscow.

JENKINS, R. (1952), 'Equality', *New Fabian Essays*, Fabian Society.

KARCZ, J. F. (1966), 'Seven years on the farm: retrospective and prospects', US Congress, Joint Economic Committee, *New Directions in the Soviet Economy*, Washington, DC: Government Printing Office, pp. 383–472.

KATUNTSEVA, N. M. (1966), *Rol' rabochikh fakul'tetov v formirovanie kadrov narodnoy intelligentsii v SSSR*, Moscow.

KHARCHEV, A. G. (1965), 'O putyakh dal'neyshego ukrepleniya sem'i v SSSR' *Sotsial'nye issledovaniya*, no. 1.

144 References

Klassy, sotsial'nye sloi i gruppy v SSSR (1968), Moscow.

KORNHAUSER, W. (1960), *The Politics of Mass Society*, Routledge & Kegan Paul.

KOSTIN, L. (1960), *Wages in the Soviet Union*, Moscow.

KROPOTKIN, Peter (1888), *The Wage System*, Freedom Press.

KPSS (1969) *Naglayadnoe posobie partiynomu stroitel'stvu*, Moscow.

KPSS (1966) *XXIII S'ezd*, vols. 1 and 2, 1966, Moscow.

'KKSS v tsifrakh (1961–1964 gody)' (1965) *Partiynaya zhizn*', no. 10, pp. 8–17.

KURON, J., and MODZELEWSKI, K. (1968), *An Open Letter to the Party*, International Socialism Publication.

LANE, D. (1969), *The Roots of Russian Communism*, Van Gorcum.

LANE, D. (1970), *Politics and Society in the USSR*, Weidenfeld & Nicolson.

LENIN, V. I. (1965), 'Economics and politics in the era of the dictatorship of the proletariat', *Collected Works*, vol. 30.

LENSKI, G. E. (1966), *Power and Privilege, A Theory of Social Stratification*, McGraw-Hill.

LIPSET, S. M. (1969), *Revolution and Counter-revolution*, Heinemann.

LOBODZINSKA, B. (1970), *Trends in the Homogeneity and Equality in Urban Marriages in Poland*, World Congress of Sociology, Varna.

LOCKWOOD, D. (1958), *The Blackcoated Worker*, Allen & Unwin.

MACHONIN, P. (1969), 'The social structure of contemporary Czechoslovak society', *Czechoslovak Economic Papers*, no. 11.

MACHONIN, P. (1970), 'Social stratification in contemporary Czechoslovakia', *Amer. J. Socio.*, vol. 75, no. 5, pp. 725–41.

MANEVICH, E. L. (1966), *Problemy obshchestvennogo truda v SSSR*, Moscow.

Marksistsko-leninskaya filosofiya i sotsiologiya v SSSR i Evropeiskikh sotsialisticheskikh stran, 1965, Moscow.

MARX, K., and ENGELS, F. (1965), *The German Ideology*, Lawrence & Wishart.

MARX, K. (1958a), 'The Eighteenth Brumaire of Louis Napoleon', Marx-Engels, *Selected Works*, vol. 1, Moscow.

MARX, K. (1958b), 'Preface to the critique of political economy', in *Selected Works*, vol. 1, Moscow.

MARX, K. (1867), reprinted 1962, *Capital*, vol. 3, Moscow.

MEISSNER, B. (1966), 'Totalitarian rule and social change', *Problems of Communism*, vol. 15, no. 6.

MEYER, A. G. (1964), 'USSR incorporated', in D. W. Treadgold (ed.), *The Development of the USSR, an Exchange of Views*, University of Washington Press.

MILLER, S. M. (1960), 'Comparative social mobility', *Current Sociology*, vol. 9, no. 1, pp. 1–62.

MIL'TYKBAEV, KH. M. (1965), *Izmenenie sotsial'noy struktury obshchestva v period razvernutogo kommunisticheskogo stroitel'stva*, Tashkent.

MÜLLER, V. (1969), 'The price of egalitariansim', *Problems of Communism*, nos. 4–5, pp. 48–9.

MUSATOV, I. M. (1967), *Sotsial'nye problemy trudovykh resursov v SSSR*, Moscow.

NOVE, A., and NEWTH, J. A. (1966), *The Soviet Middle East, A Model for Development*, Allen & Unwin.

OSIPOV, G. V., and FROLOV, S. F. (1966), 'Vnerabochee vremya i ego ispol'zovania', *Sotsiologiya v SSSR*, vol. 2, Moscow, pp. 225–42.

OSSOWSKI, S. (1963), *Class Structure in the Social Consciousness*, Routledge & Kegan Paul.

PARKIN, F. (1969), 'Class stratification in socialist societies', *Brit. J. Soc.*, vol. 20, no. 4.

PARKIN, F. (1971), *Class Inequality and Political Order, Social Stratification in Capitalist and Communist Societies*, MacGibbon & Kee.

PARSONS, T. (1954), 'An analytical approach to the theory of social stratification' in *Essays in Sociological Theory*, rev. edn., Free Press, pp. 69–88.

POD'YACHICH, P. G. (1961), *Naselenie SSSR*, Moscow.

Problemy izmeneniya sotsial'noy struktury Sovetskogo obshchestve, 1968, Moscow.

The Programme of the Communist Party of the Soviet Union (1961), Soviet Booklet, no. 83, London.

Prostessy izmeneniya sotsial'noy struktury v Sovetskom obshchestve (1967), Sverdlovsk.

RASHIN, A. G. (1961), 'Dinamika promyshlennykh kadrov SSSR za 1917–1958 gg.', *Izmeneniya v chislennosti i sostave Sovetskogo rabochego klassa*, Moscow.

RIDDELL, D. (1968), 'Social self-government: the background of theory and practice in Yugoslav socialism', *Brit. J. Sociol.*, vol. 19.

RIGBY, T. H. (1968), *Communist Party Membership in the USSR: 1917–67*, Princeton University Press.

RIZZI, B. (1939), *La Bureaucratisation du Monde*, Paris.

ROGACHEV, P. M., and SVERDLIN, M. A. (1966), 'O ponyatii "Natsiya"', *Voprosy istorii*, no. 1.

ROSSI, P. H., and INKELES, A. (1957), 'Multidimensional ratings of occupations', *Sociometry*, vol. 20, no. 3.

SADOWSKI, M. (1968), 'Przemiany spoleczne a partie politiczne PRL', *Studia Sociologiczne*, no. 30–31.

SAFAR, Z. *et al.* (1970), *Basic Data on Social Differentiation in the Czechoslovak Socialist Society*. Varna: World Congress of Sociology.

SAIFULIN, M. (ed.) (1967), *The Soviet Parliament*, Progress Publishers.

SARAPATA, A. (1966), 'Stratification and social mobility' in Jan Szczepanski (ed.), *Empirical Sociology in Poland*, Warsaw, Polish Scientific Publishers, pp. 37–52.

SCHACHTMAN, M. (1962), *The Bureaucratic Revolution*, Donald Press.

SCHAPIRO, L. (1960), *The Communist Party of the Soviet Union*, Constable.

SCHLESINGER, R. (1956), *The Nationalities Problem and Soviet Administration*, Routledge & Kegan Paul.

SCHNELLER, G. K. (1966), 'The Politburo', in H. D. Lasswell and D. Lerner (eds.), *World Revolutionary Elites, Studies in Coercive Ideological Movements*, M.I.T. Press, pp. 97–178.

SEMENOV, V. S. (1962), 'Preobrazovaniya v rabochem klasse i intelligentsii v protsesse perekhoda k kommunizmu', *Ot sotsializma k kommunizmu*, Moscow.

SEMENOV, V. S. (1964), 'O partii i intelligentsii v Sovetskom Soyuze', *Marksistskaya i burzhuaznaya sotsiologiya segodnya*, Moscow, pp. 254–63.

SEMENOV, V. S. (1968), 'Rabochi klass-vedushchaya sila Sovetskogo obshchestva', *Klassy, sotsial'nye sloi i gruppy v SSSR*, Moscow.

SHKARATAN, O. I. (1967), 'Sotsial'naya struktura Sovetskogo rabochego klassa', *Voprosy filosofii*, no. 1, pp. 28–39.

SHMELEV, G. (1965), 'Ekonomicheskaya rol' lichnogo podsobnogo khozyaystva', *Voprosy ekonomiki* no. 4, pp. 27–37.

SHTRAKS, G. M. (1966), *Sotsial'noe edinstvo i protivorechiya sotsialisticheskogo obshchestva*, Moscow.

SHUBKIN, V. N. (1965), 'Molodezh' vstupaet v zhizn'', *Voprosy filosofii*, no. 5, pp. 57–70.

SHUBKIN, V. N. (1966), 'Social mobility and choice of occupation', in G. V. Osipov (ed.), *Industry and Labour in the USSR*, Tavistock, pp. 86–98.

SIK, O. (1967), *Plan and Market under Socialism*, International Arts and Sciences Press.

SKILLING, H. G. (1966), *The Governments of Communist East Europe*, Crowell.

SMIRNOV, G. (1965), 'Dinamika rosta rabochego klassa i izmenenie ego professional'nogo-kvalifikatsionnogo sostava' in *Sotsiologiya v SSSR*, vol. 1, Moscow.

SLOMCZYNSKI, K. (1970), *Socio-Occupational Differentiation and Education, Authority, Income and Prestige*, Varna, World Congress of Sociology.

STALIN, I. V. (1952), *Economic Problems of Socialism*, Moscow Foreign Languages Publishing House.

STALIN, I. V. (1955), 'Talk with Emil Ludwig', *Collected Works*, vol. 13, Moscow, 1955.

STALIN, I. V. (1967), 'O proekte konstitutsii Soyuza SSSR', *Sochineniya*, vol. 1 (24), Stanford University Press for the Hoover Institute.

STEWART, P. D. (1968), *Political Power in the Soviet Union*, Bobbs-Merrill.

Struktura Sovetskoy intelligentsii (1970), Minsk.

SUKHAREVSKI, B. M. (1968), 'Zarabotnaya plata i material'naya zainterovannost't', *Trud i zarabotnaya plata v SSSR*, Moscow.

Szesztay, A. (1967), *Veszprèmben végeztek*, Budapest.

Skilling, H. G., and Griffiths, F. (1971), *Interest Groups in Soviet Politics*, Princeton University Press.

Tkach, Ya. M. (1967), 'Roditeli o sud'bakh svoikh detey', *Protsessy izmeneniya sotsial'noy struktury v sovetskom obshchestve*, Sverdlovsk.

Trotsky, L. (1945), *The Revolution Betrayed: the Soviet Union, what it is and where it is going*, Pioneer.

Trud v SSSR (1968) Moscow.

Tsentral'noe statisticheskoe upravlenie (1962), *Itogi vsesoyuznoy perepisi naseleniya 1959g. SSSR (svodny tom)*, Moscow.

Tsentral'noe (1963), *Narodnoe khozyaystvo SSSR v 1962g*, Moscow.

Tsentral'noe (1966), *Narodnoe khozyaystvo SSSR v 1965g*, Moscow.

Tsentral'noe (1967), *Strana Sovetov za 50 let: sbornik statisticheskikh materialov*, Moscow.

Tsentral'noe (1969), *Narodnoe khozyaystvo SSSR v 1968g*, Moscow.

Tsentral'noe (1970), *Narodnoe khozyaystvo SSSR v 1969g*, Moscow.

Tumin, M. M. (1964), 'Ethnic groups', in J. Gould and W. L. Kolb (eds.), *A Dictionary of the Social Sciences*, Tavistock.

United Nations (1967), *Economic Survey of Europe in 1965*, Geneva.

Vol'fson, S. Ya. (1937), *Sem'ya i Brak*, Moscow.

Voritsyn, S. (1969), 'The present composition of the party central committee: a brief sociological analysis', *Bulletin of the Institute for the Study of the USSR*, vol. 26.

Wesolowski, W. (1966), 'Changes in the class structure in Poland' in J. Szczepanski (ed.), *Empirical Sociology in Poland*, Warsaw, Polish Scientific Publications, pp. 7–35.

Wesolowski, W. (1969), 'The notions of strata and class in socialist society' in A. Béteille (ed.), *Social Inequality*, Penguin.

Wheeler, G. (1964), *The Modern History of Soviet Central Asia*, Weidenfeld & Nicolson.

Widerszpil, S. *et al*. (1959), 'Do jakiej klassy na ezysz?' *Zycie Gospodarcze*, no. 25, p. 1–4.

Wiles, P. J. D., and Markowski, S. (1971), 'Income distribution under Communism and Capitalism; some facts about Poland, the UK, the USA and the USSR', *Soviet Studies*, vol. 22, no. 3, pp. 344–69.

Woodcock, G. (1962), *Anarchism*, World Publishing Co; Penguin, 1963.

Zagorski, K. (1970), *Social Mobility and Changes in the Structure of Planning Society*, Warsaw.

'Zhenshchiny v SSSR', 1965, *Vestnik statistiki* no. 2.

Zhenshchiny i deti v SSSR (1969), Moscow.

Index

Penguin Modern Sociology Readings

The Ecology of Human Intelligence
Edited by Liam Hudson

Industrial Man
Edited by Tom Burns

Peasants and Peasant Societies
Edited by Teodor Shanin

Social Inequality
Edited by André Betaille

Sociology of Law
Edited by Wilhelm Aubert

Sociology of Religion
Edited by Roland Robertson

Sociology of the Family
Edited by Michael Anderson

Witchcraft and Sorcery
Edited by Max Marwick

Introducing Sociology

Edited by Peter Worsley and members of the Department of Social Anthropology and Sociology, University of Manchester.

Sociology is now a major area of intellectual inquiry in most countries of the world. It is also seen by an increasing number of its students as one of the most relevant of contemporary disciplines.

Introducing Sociology is an exciting and wholly original text which acknowledges both these points. It is, first and foremost, an introduction to sociological ideas and practice, not an exhaustive summary. It is written in a style which, at no sacrifice of scientific rigour, is refreshingly free from jargon. Its subject-matter is drawn from the common life-experience of most people born into the mid-twentieth century. Indeed the examples used in the book have been deliberately chosen from a wide range of cultures and societies to underline the international roots and relevance of modern sociology.

Published as a companion volume is *Modern Sociology: Introductory Readings*, prepared by the same team.